Once There Was, Twice There Wasn't

Once There Was, Twice There Wasn't

Fifty Turkish Folktales of Nasreddin Hodja

Adapted by Michael Shelton

Hey Nonny Nonny Press
BOSTON

First published in the United States in 2014 by
Hey Nonny Nonny Press

ISBN-13: 978-0692026564 (paperback)
ISBN-10: 0692026568 (paperback)

Book design and type formatting by Lori A. Cook

Manufactured in the United States of America

Then sigh not so, but let them go,
And be you blithe and bonny;
Converting all your sounds of woe
Into Hey nonny nonny!

William Shakespeare, *Much Ado About Nothing*

For Joann,
my beloved helpmate and best cheerleader.

And for Kate, Rebekah, Grace, Joy, Hope, and Faith,
my first and favorite audience for these tales.

I love you all more than words can tell.

Contents

Contents

Preface

Nasreddin Hodja stories are told in teahouses from China to Hungary and from southern Siberia to North Africa. The Arabs know him as the clever Joha. To the people of Egypt, he is the prankster Goha. To the people of China, he is the wise Affanti. The people of Turkey, however, claim the historical figure behind the legendary folk hero.

Nasreddin Hodja was born the son of an imam in 1208 in Horto village near Sivrihisar in the Turkish heartland of Central Anatolia. His given name, Nasr-ed-Din means "Victory of the Faith." He later acquired the honorific title "hodja," meaning "master" or "teacher."

As an adult, Nasreddin Hodja may have served as a judge, an imam, a teacher, and a dervish. He is thought to have died in 1284 in Akshehir. You can visit his tomb, which is guarded by a locked gate without walls, symbolizing the absurdity he loved to poke fun at in life.

The story is told in Turkey that one day, a friend found Nasreddin Hodja pouring a small bowl of yogurt into the lake.

"Nasreddin Hodja, what are you doing?" the man asked.

"I am turning the lake into yogurt."

"But Hodja, a little bit of yeast cannot ferment an entire lake!"

"You never know," Nasreddin Hodja answered with a grin, "What if it can?"

This simple collection of traditional folktales can scarcely begin to introduce the reader to the riches of the Turkish culture I have grown to love. However, inspired by Nasreddin Hodja's eternal optimism, by retelling some of my favorite tales here I have dared to ask, "What if it can?"

Allah'a bin shukur, a thousand praises to God, for my dear friends and neighbors, Hanefi and Ayten Yoloğlu, who first introduced me to many of the tales in this book. Special thanks also to the multitude of Turkish brothers and sisters, uncles and aunts, market sellers, neighbors, and the patrons of a hundred teahouses who have enthusiastically enlarged my acquaintance with the remarkable Nasreddin Hodja and his exploits. I am likewise grateful to Allyson Baldwin for proofreading this manuscript and for her many encouragements toward its completion.

Thank you to Lori Cook for the interior design of this volume.

Thanks to my kind editor and publisher Patricia Anders for putting this book into print.

Michael Shelton

The Contest and the Candle

ne bitter winter night, Nasreddin Hodja and his friends gathered together at the local teahouse. As they warmed themselves with glasses of hot tea, small talk about the weather gave way to boasting.

"This cold is nothing compared to the winters of my home village of Horto," Hodja bragged. "As a young man, I used to break the ice on the pond to take a brisk bath on a day like this. Cold is not a problem for a hot-blooded young man like me."

"Come, Hodja," his friends laughed indulgently, "not even the hot air of your boasts could keep you warm on a night like this."

Spurred on by their mockery Hodja answered, "You call this cold? I could stay out all night long in this weather without even a coat."

Winking at his companions, one man asked, "No fire, no hot tea, no blanket?" When Hodja nodded, everyone in the teahouse seemed impressed.

"Well then, Hodja," said another, "let's make a bargain. If you can stay outside for the entire night with nothing to warm you, each of us will host you in turn for a fine dinner. But if you fail, you will entertain all twelve of us at your house for dinner. Agreed?"

When Hodja realized that he could not back down without losing face, he agreed to the terms and stepped out into the chill evening.

Throughout the night, his friends kept watch through the windows of their warm houses as Hodja paced back and forth through the village square, rubbing his arms and cursing his hasty tongue. Hodja's faithful wife Ayten lit a yellow candle in their window and waved to Hodja from time to time to support him through his frosty vigil.

When at last the sun crept above the horizon, Nasreddin Hodja shuffled stiffly back to the teahouse to find his friends waiting. It was a long time before Hodja's teeth stopped chattering enough for him to ask, "Who will be the first to invite me to dinner?"

"Actually, Hodja effendi," they responded grinning, "it is we who will be eating at your house tonight since you lost the wager. We all saw the yellow candle in your window. Surely you must have warmed yourself by that candle."

"That's nonsense!" Hodja protested. "How could a candle behind a window two hundred feet away keep a man warm?"

But when Hodja saw that his friends were unmoved by the justice of his argument, he graciously submitted to their majority and invited them all to dinner at his house that night.

The whole group arrived early at Nasreddin Hodja's home in high spirits. When Hodja excused himself to check on the dinner preparations, they congratulated one another on outwitting the remarkable Hodja. As minutes passed into hours without any sign of the promised feast, their gloating gave way to impatience and they began to grumble to Hodja about the delay.

"Fear not my friends," their host responded genially. "Come and see for yourselves that your dinner is being made ready." The hungry group followed Hodja into the kitchen where they were amazed to find a large cauldron filled with rice hanging from the ceiling above a yellow candle.

"Have you gone mad, Hodja?" the men cried in frustration. "You can't expect to heat that cauldron with a candle. The dinner will never be cooked."

"But friends," Hodja replied in mock surprise, "it is you who have persuaded me that it is possible. If this candle can warm a man two hundred feet away, surely it can heat up a cauldron two inches away."

Honest Hands

 young boy burst into the teahouse and yelled, "Hasan is going to be executed!" Men leaped to their feet in shock, overturning glasses of hot tea. Others shouted questions over one another and called down curses on Emperor Tamerlane.

Despite the confusion, the story was quickly told. Hasan had been caught stealing bread from the bakery by one of the Emperor's own soldiers. Emperor Tamerlane had already condemned him to a public execution.

Hasan was a poor and decent man who never stole but from hunger. Hasan had a wife and eight children. Hasan was Nasreddin Hodja's cousin. For all these reasons Hasan had his countrymen's sympathy. Nevertheless, there was little any of them could do but grumble into their tea about the unjust severity of his punishment. Hodja thumbed through a worn string of prayer beads, his eyes closed in deep thought.

Hodja's friends noted his silence and tried to comfort him. "Come, Hodja," they said. "We know Hasan is a relative of yours but that your hands are empty in this matter. There is nothing you can do."

Nasreddin Hodja's eyes flew open at their words. "On the contrary, in my hands I have all that I need." Then he rose and visited the miserable Hasan in his prison cell. There Hodja quietly explained to his cousin what he must do.

The next day, Emperor Tamerlane and his retinue took seats behind the executioner's block to enjoy the spectacle and were pleased to see that a crowd from the town had gathered. As Hasan was brought forward in chains, he suddenly reached into his pocket and called out, "Wait! I have a gift for the Emperor!" The Emperor and his advisors were curious. No condemned man had ever said such a thing before. They all leaned forward to see what Hasan was holding in his hand.

"My lord," Hasan continued, "let me die this day if your justice demands, but do not let this precious treasure pass from the world."

Now everyone in the crowd was staring curiously at the string of beads in Hasan's hand.

"These are no ordinary beads," Hasan said in answer to their unspoken question. "They come from a holy dervish in the distant East who vowed to me that in the hands of a truly honest man they will turn into a string of diamonds. They are of no use to a thief like me, so I give them to you, my just lord." And Hasan offered the worn string of beads to Tamerlane.

Emperor Tamerlane hesitated. If he accepted the beads, everyone would be watching to see if they turned into diamonds in his hands. He remembered lands he had taken, innocent men he had condemned, and alliances he had broken. His were not honest hands.

But if he did not accept the beads, the people would guess the reason. What could he do? The crowd was already starting to murmur when the aged voice of Nasreddin Hodja called out, "Our generous Emperor wishes to show mercy!"

In a flash, Emperor Tamerlane saw what he must do. He raised his hand for silence and called out, "I cannot accept such a gift from one who may yet prove worthy of it. I hearby reduce your penalty to one month's labor for the baker you have stolen from. Who knows but that honest labor may give you honest hands and I have diamonds enough."

As the people cheered at this uncharacteristic display of wisdom and mercy from their harsh ruler, the Emperor, Hodja, and Hasan all sighed in relief: the Emperor for his honor, Hodja for his family, and Hasan for his life. It is said that Hasan turned out to be such a good worker that the baker not only forgave him his desperate theft but also hired him on permanently. In time, Hasan built a thriving bakery of his own to pass on to his sons.

As for the beads, Hasan returned them to his wise cousin. When his friends asked if the beads were truly magical, Hodja smiled and answered, "Who can say? For there are no flawless servants of Allah with which to put them to the test."

The Guest of Honor

asreddin Hodja was famished. It was Ramazan, the month of fasting when faithful Muslims are forbidden to eat or drink from sunrise to sunset. Fortunately, Hodja had been invited to *iftar*, the breaking of the fast, at the home of the local muhtar. Sweating in his fields under the hot sun, Nasreddin Hodja consoled his grumbling stomach with the promise of fine food and good company at the muhtar's table.

Hunger and thirst slowed Hodja's steps, however, and he arrived home just in time to see the sun reaching down to touch the horizon. "It would be shameful to keep my host waiting on this auspicious night," Hodja said to himself. He ran straight to the muhtar's house without stopping to change out of his sweaty work clothes.

When he arrived at the muhtar's courtyard, Hodja walked confidently among the assembled guests. He tossed greetings to the left and the right and was so relieved to arrive on time that he did not at once notice that he was talking to backs instead of faces. Nasreddin Hodja's polite smiles were ignored and his words fell to the ground unheeded.

When the voice of the muezzin echoed down from the minaret, the muhtar ushered his honored guests to the table. Meanwhile, one of the servants mistook Hodja for a beggar and directed him discreetly to a dark corner of the floor.

Nasreddin Hodja cleared his throat noisily to draw his host's attention to his unfortunate position. But the muhtar paid no heed to beggars. Hodja coughed loudly. But the muhtar seemed unable to see or hear the one guest who sat alone on the floor in his dirty work clothes.

"My muhtar!" Hodja called out cheerfully. "*Kesene bereket!* May Allah bless your purse for sharing this fine feast."

What a feast! Mountains of steaming rice pilav with chickpeas, savory strips of grilled lamb, cool yogurt *cacik* with cucumber and mint, oven-fresh *pide* breads, juicy dates stuffed with walnuts, and other choice foods circulated through the tables. However, by the time they reached the ravenous Hodja, the trays were emptied of all but scraps and crusts.

Nasreddin Hodja looked thoughtfully at the well-scrubbed and adorned guests around the table. Then he considered his dirt-caked hands and patched work clothes. Finally, he left his unused plate and quietly slipped back to his home.

"Hot water, Ayten!" he called. "Soap, Ayten! My best turban! My new coat!"

Ayten shined Nasreddin Hodja's shoes and laid out his finest clothes while he bathed and scrubbed himself from top to toe. Soon he looked like a new man. Hodja preened before an admiring Ayten, who had not seen her husband so well groomed in years.

"Husband, you would grace the court of the Emperor himself," she said with approval.

With this encouragement, Hodja swaggered out of the house. Young men ducked their heads deferentially as he strutted back down the street to the muhtar's house.

When Hodja arrived in his finery, a servant hurried forward to escort him into the muhtar's feast. A hush fell over the room as a beaming muhtar rose from his seat to kiss the back of Nasreddin Hodja's hand and lead him straight to the place of honor at his own tray. One guest after another vied for Hodja's comment and advice while the muhtar directed the choicest delicacies to his plate.

But the muhtar's welcome turned to astonishment when he saw Nasreddin Hodja begin stuffing grilled meatballs into the pocket of his handsome coat. "Eat, my master!" Hodja said. Then he tipped a plate full of eggplant into another pocket. "Eat, my lord!"

First the muhtar, then the guests, then the servants stared in shock, but no one could make any sense of Hodja's bizarre behavior. Finally, the muhtar blurted out, "Hodja effendi, what on earth are you doing?"

"I am surprised you ask," Hodja replied innocently. "Since you all ignored me until I put on this fancy coat, it seems clear that it was my coat who was invited to this banquet and not me. Therefore, I am feeding the coat."

Those Who Know

n the days before clocks and calendars conspired to cage the hearts of men, Nasreddin Hodja fluttered through his days like a leaf on the wind. Six days a week he could haggle in the marketplace or work in the fields. He could swap stories over hot tea with his friends or take long walks in the woods or nap in the sunshine. Six days a week he did what he pleased when he pleased without hurry or responsibility.

Only Friday was different. On Fridays his carefree hours were leashed by duty. For it is on Friday that every good Muslim attends mosque to listen to their local imam preach. As the most educated and eloquent man in his neighborhood, the honor fell to Nasreddin Hodja to mount the stairs of the minber each Friday and preach to the community.

Now it is true that Hodja got on very well at first, for he was a man of many opinions that wanted airing. But even the deepest well can run dry. As the weeks wore into months and years, Hodja found it increasingly difficult to find fresh things to say. It was one thing to laugh over tales at the teahouse but quite another to look down into the solemn faces of the men squatting on their prayer rugs and think of a suitable sermon each week.

"After all, our faith is simplicity itself," Hodja mused. "Speak the confession, 'There is no God but Allah and Mohammed is His Messenger,' perform the ritual prayers five times a day, fast during Ramazan, make the pilgrimage to Mecca, and give alms. How much more is there to say?"

Yet each Friday, Hodja was obligated to supply some new insight or reflection to improve upon these simple instructions.

Finally, one Friday Nasreddin Hodja's mind was as blank as fresh parchment when the cantillating call of the muezzin echoed down from the minaret, summoning all good believers to the mosque. Veiled women wove modestly through the streets on their way to their screened balcony in the mosque. What would he say to them today? Hodja joined the men at their ablutions in the mosque courtyard, washing his body while he wracked his brains. What could he say?

Hodja left his sandals among the rows of shoes at the mosque entrance and padded quietly across the deep carpets within. While the men squatted down in lines facing Mecca, Hodja looked around at the colorfully patterned tiles decorating the walls, hoping for some last-minute inspiration. Nothing came.

When he could delay no longer, Nasreddin Hodja ascended the stairs of the minber and then turned to face the assembled congregation. He glanced longingly out the window at the sunny spring day outside and then down at the mens' faces staring expectantly up at him. He heard the faint stirrings from the latticed balcony above where veiled women sat hidden from view. He knew he must say something.

"Oh, people of Akshehir!" Nasreddin Hodja cried out in frustration to the gathered assembly. "Do you know what I am going say to you today?"

Rows of curious faces looked up in surprise at Hodja's question. Suddenly he understood what he must do.

"No! We don't know," the men answered uncertainly from below.

Hodja shook his head in disappointment. "If you do not know, then I will not waste the fountain of my eloquence on desert sand. I have nothing to say to the ignorant."

With that, the Hodja turned and climbed down the steps. His eyes lowered, he walked with injured dignity through the stunned crowd. He slipped on his sandals at the mosque door and escaped into the sunshine—free for another week.

The next Friday came all too soon. Hodja again mingled with the crowds surging toward the mosque. He ascended the minber and surveyed the sea of solemn faces below him. He heard the rustling whisper of veils behind the screened balcony above.

"Oh, people of Akshehir!" Hodja intoned. "Do you know what I am going to say to you today?"

"Yes," boomed the men in unison for they had not forgotten the previous week.

"If you already know," Hodja responded with a shrug, "then I have nothing more to add but to thank Allah for your enlightenment."

Then Hodja turned and stepped down from the minber. Humming to himself, he threaded his way with unhurried dignity through the seated men and out into the waiting sunshine. Another free week was ahead of him.

On the third Friday, Nasreddin Hodja once more climbed the carved steps to face the congregation. All eyes were fixed on him when he asked the familiar question.

"People of Akshehir!" Hodja called, "do you know what I am going to say to you today?"

This time the people were determined to get a sermon out of Hodja and had prepared their answer in advance. Half of them cried out "We know!" while the other half said "We don't know!"

Hodja smiled and clapped his hands together. "In that case let those who know teach those who do not!"

With that, Hodja bounced down from the minber, two steps at a time. He nodded and smiled as he slipped back through the crowd and picked up his sandals from the rows by the mosque entrance. He whistled as he walked out into another inviting spring day. The birds were chirping in praise of Allah's beautiful creation and Hodja was free to enjoy it all without duty or care.

At least until the next Friday.

The Backward Seat

 asreddin Hodja had a tall turban but a short memory and was prone to forgetting what he was doing while pondering some weighty matter. Nevertheless, the quick-witted Hodja managed to turn even such missteps to his advantage. Such was the case when a delegation from a neighboring village came knocking on his front door one day, *tik tik tik.*

"*Selamunaleykum*, peace be with you, Hodja effendi," said the eldest as he kissed Nasreddin Hodja's hand and pressed it to his forehead. "Our village needs a new imam and we have been searching for someone worthy to be our spiritual guide. We have come to invite you to return with us so that the village can see if the reports of your wisdom are true."

Nasreddin Hodja needed the job and was anxious to live up to his reputation. He quickly put on his long coat and his tall turban. Then Hodja slipped into his shoes at the doorstep and hurried out to the stable to mount his little donkey. Unfortunately, Hodja's thoughts had already rushed ahead to his new position, leaving his feet to fend for themselves. He suddenly looked down and realized that he had mounted his donkey backward!

The villagers looked at one another skeptically. Could this be the famous Hodja they had come to hire? How could he lead the namaz prayers if he could not even mount his own donkey?

Hodja read the concern in their eyes and so drew up his dignity and spoke swiftly to dispel their doubts.

"You may be wondering," Hodja said, "why I have chosen to sit backward on my donkey. Be assured that I have good reason. If I were to seat myself forward on my donkey and ride ahead of you, my back would be turned toward you and that would be discourteous.

"On the other hand, if I were to sit forward on the donkey and ride behind you, that would be shameful, for I am your spiritual leader. But seated this way, I can ride ahead of you *and* face toward you."

The men from the village had never considered the matter in such a way and marveled at Hodja's penetrating insight. They agreed together then and there that they had found a worthy imam for their village.

This story and its many variations are so well known in Turkey that Nasreddin Hodja is most often depicted riding backwards on a donkey.

A Reason for Praise

asreddin Hodja loved nothing better than to play the host and fill his home with guests who would compliment him on his wife's fine cooking and give audience to his jokes and stories. What is money for but spending and sharing? Unfortunately, Hodja's resources never quite matched his generosity.

"Hospitality is a virtue, husband," his wife Ayten cautioned him one day. "But open hands require a full pot and I have nothing left to set before any guests but plums from our tree."

Now Nasreddin Hodja was inordinately proud of those plums. He was certain that there were no better plums in all Akshehir. Why they were fit for the Emperor himself! And that gave Hodja an idea.

Hodja went out to his garden and picked several of the largest purple plums. "If generosity has brought me into trouble, perhaps it can bring me out," he thought to himself as he stacked the plums onto a copper tray and set off for the Emperor's palace.

By chance, Emperor Tamerlane was in excellent humor when Hodja arrived. He was received with all the courtesy due to an honored guest. When Hodja presented his gift, the Emperor vowed that he had never tasted sweeter plums. They sat down together on stuffed cushions and Tamerlane ate and laughed at Hodja's jokes until the plums were gone.

When Hodja at last rose to leave, Tamerlane begged him to accept a gift in return. The Emperor refilled Hodja's tray with gold coins. So it was that Nasreddin Hodja returned home with a full purse, well pleased with his day.

That satisfaction and the coins that came with it lasted Nasreddin Hodja for some time. But at last the day came when Ayten's cupboards were once more bare, and Hodja decided it was time to visit Emperor Tamerlane again.

"What gift shall I bring the great man this time?" Hodja mused as he looked at his empty tray. The plums were no longer in season but perhaps there was another suitable gift in the garden?

"What about some good red beets?" he wondered, still staring at the empty tray. "Yes, beets will be just the thing."

Hodja went into the garden and collected some of his reddest, firmest beets. He arranged these on the tray, balanced the tray on his head, and started off toward the road.

"Where are you taking those beets, husband?" asked Ayten.

"These beets are a gift for Emperor Tamerlane," Hodja replied.

"You are bringing beets to the Emperor?" she said, clucking her tongue.

"Aren't beets a suitable gift?" Hodja took the tray from his head and looked at the beets as though for the first time. They did not seem quite as magnificent as when he was pulling them. "Perhaps something else would be better?"

"You know best, husband," Ayten answered gently, "but perhaps the Emperor would favor some juicy figs fresh from the tree?"

"Of course, something sweet to sweeten his mood!" Why had he not thought of that? Nasreddin Hodja hurried off to the bazaar where he traded his firm red beets for a tray of juicy, ripe figs.

"You are fortunate," the fig seller told him, "to get so many luscious figs for a few common beets." But behind these honeyed words the merchant thought to himself, "I am lucky to rid myself of those overripe figs. They were so soft that I was just about to throw them away."

Pleased with his bargain, Nasreddin Hodja hurried on to Tamerlane's court. He hoped to find the Emperor in another generous mood but a different fate was written on his forehead. The Emperor's worries were many that morning, and his mood was as black as a moonless night. When he saw Hodja's platter of overripe figs, he flew into a rage.

"How dare you bring me rotten fruit!" Tamerlane roared. It felt good to vent his anger on someone and at once the Emperor thought of a fitting punishment.

"Guards!" he shouted. "Take this fool's figs and throw them at him! Throw every single one of them at him! And throw them hard!"

Hodja tried to run away, but the soldiers surrounded him and pelted him with the squishy figs. Smack! Splosh! Squish! Spatter! The figs exploded across the back of Hodja's best robe as he cowered beneath the fruity assault. Then he cried out,

"Thank you, Allah, the Compassionate and Merciful. A thousand praises!"

Emperor Tamerlane stared at Hodja in surprise and motioned for his men to pause in their attack.

"What do you mean by giving thanks, Hodja?" Tamerlane demanded. "You have been humiliated."

"Yes, my lord," Hodja answered, "but Allah be praised that I did not bring you my hard red beets or else my bones would have been broken as well!"

The sight of Nasreddin Hodja bespattered with sticky seeds made Tamerlane grin despite himself. He realized that Hodja had spoken wisely. Indeed a cloud lifted from his heart when he saw that he too could find a reason for praise in that his own troubles could also be far worse.

The Emperor helped Hodja to his feet. "Come my wise fool of a Hodja," he said with a smile. "You may have no eye for figs, but you have lightened my burdens today and for that at least you deserve some reward."

Then Tamerlane pressed a purse of gold into Hodja's sticky hands and sent him on his way. May we all share in his good fortune.

"A thousand friends are too few. One enemy is too many."
—Turkish proverb

Duck Soup

distant relative visited Nasreddin Hodja from the East and brought him a plump duck for dinner. Delighted with this unexpected bounty, Hodja roasted the bird and shared it with his guest.

Soon after his relative left, a stranger arrived at Hodja's doorstep. He identified himself as a friend "of the man who gave you the duck." Hodja was, of course, obligated to offer him hospitality according to the laws of Allah and his prophet.

In the weeks that followed, a steady stream of visitors found their way to Nasreddin Hodja's door, each of them claiming some relation to the original donor of the duck. Finally, Hodja's patience was strained to the breaking point. He resolved to get the best of those who would treat his home like an inn and so abuse his hospitality.

The next day another stranger knocked at the door and announced that he was "the friend of the friend of the friend of the man who brought you the duck." Nasreddin Hodja welcomed him warmly and ushered him inside to the table. Then he seated his guest at the place of honor and motioned for his wife Ayten to bring the soup.

The guest eagerly tasted the soup but found that it was nothing more than warm water. Disappointed, the visitor asked "What sort of soup is this, Hodja effendi?"

"My friend," said Nasreddin Hodja, "it is the soup of the soup of the soup of the duck."

"The guest eats what he finds, not what he hopes for."
—Turkish proverb

Servant of the Eggplant

t one time, Nasreddin Hodja was a favorite of Emperor Tamerlane and often dined with him at the palace. One day the palace chef served the Emperor a savory eggplant dish. The Emperor enjoyed it so much that he ordered the same dish to be served to him every day.

"Is not this eggplant the best of vegetables, Hodja?" Emperor Tamerlane asked.

"Yes, Your Majesty," Hodja replied. "It is a prince among vegetables, the noblest of Allah's garden, a blessing to the tongue."

After several days, however, Emperor Tamerlane lost his taste for eggplant. When the same eggplant dish was served for the tenth straight meal, the Emperor roared, "Take this food away! It's awful!"

"Yes, Your Majesty," Hodja agreed. "It is a wretched vegetable, a stain on Allah's garden, a curse to the tongue."

"But Hodja, just a few days ago you said that it was a blessing to the tongue!"

"Yes, Your Majesty. But I am the servant of the Emperor, not of the eggplant."

Hodja's Recipe

 s snow falls on the highest mountains, so does folly fall on the highest officials. Or so it seemed to Nasreddin Hodja when the new muhtar made his strange proposal to the villagers of Horto.

"My countryman," the muhtar said, "surely you have noticed that the first fresh fruits and vegetables of each season command the highest prices. Therefore, this year let us sow our crops a month early to reap an earlier and more profitable harvest."

The crowd buzzed in admiration of the muhtar's clever plan. Nasreddin Hodja, however, feared disaster. The muhtar may have been a persuasive speaker but he had never farmed a day in his life! When the village harvest failed because of premature planting, Horto would go hungry and it would be too late for regrets. Nevertheless, Hodja dared not oppose a powerful man like the muhtar to his face.

"My friends," Hodja spoke up, "I propose that we all think well on our muhtar's excellent proposal and make a decision tomorrow."

"In honor of this momentous day," he continued, "let me to share with you my special recipe." And Hodja went on to explain how certain quantities of honey, garlic, and boiled fish could be combined to make a delicious meal.

The crowd dispersed to their homes where not a few decided to try Hodja's recipe.

When the villagers gathered in the square again the next day, many complained loudly to Nasreddin Hodja that his recipe tasted terrible.

"What do you mean by convincing us to try that wretched recipe, Hodja?" one demanded.

"I can't get the awful taste out of my mouth," complained another.

"My friends," Hodja answered, "I confess I have never tried the recipe myself, but it seemed like such a good idea to me that I proposed it to you."

"Only a fool would recommend a recipe he had never tried himself," the villagers mocked.

"Or accept a recipe he knows is untried," Hodja added.

These last words left many farmers stroking their beards thoughtfully as they considered the muhtar's fine-sounding proposal from a new perspective. A spoiled dinner was one thing but a ruined harvest was quite another. In the end, the new farming plan was voted down. Hodja's reputation as a cook never recovered, but the village farms were saved.

The Bargain

 asreddin Hodja had a tall turban but a short purse. Perhaps that is why he loved nothing better than to bargain and haggle whenever he had a few coins. And sometimes even when he didn't.

One day Hodja went to the bazaar and chose a baggy pair of trousers. Hodja pointed out flaws in the fabric while the seller praised the tailoring as they drank tea together and haggled over the price. Finally, they clasped hands and Hodja had the merchant wrap up the trousers for purchase. But when the merchant returned with the parcel, Hodja changed his mind and decided that he wanted a new robe instead.

After several more glasses of tea, Nasreddin Hodja and the merchant agreed on a price for a fine robe and he had the merchant wrap it up. When the parcel was ready, Hodja picked it up and walked off.

"Hodja effendi," called the merchant, "you have not paid me for that robe!"

"But I left you the trousers in exchange," replied Hodja.

"You did not pay for the trousers either," said the merchant.

"I should think not!" said Hodja indignantly. "Why should I pay for trousers I did not take?"

The Judge's Turban

ne night the kadi of Sivrihisar got very drunk and stumbled down into a ditch at the side of the road. Unable to climb out, he threw off his fine new turban and passed out in the mud.

Nasreddin Hodja happened to pass by on the same road and found the snoring kadi. He picked up his unguarded turban and continued on his way.

When the kadi finally came to his senses, he hurried home and ordered his servants to search the town for the missing turban. Hodja was found wearing the turban and was brought before the kadi.

"Is that your turban?" demanded the angry kadi.

"No, sir," replied Hodja politely.

"Then what is it doing in your possession?"

"Well, sir," Hodja explained, "last night I was walking down the road on the outskirts of town, when I came across a sight disgusting to all good Muslims. Some sinful man was dead drunk and sleeping in a ditch. I was afraid that thieves would steal the valuable turban he had flung aside in his intoxicated state. I will gladly return the turban as soon as this man can be found *inshallah*."

"Who knows what a dreadful character he must be to make such a spectacle of himself," interrupted the kadi quickly. "I want nothing more to do with this matter!" And thus the kadi held on to his honor while saying farewell to his turban.

The Well of Wisdom

usband! Husband!" Ayten cried as she burst through the front door. "Wall up your heart to protect it from my bad news, for disaster is falling on our heads!"

"*Allah Korusun,* may Allah protect us!" Hodja answered as he tugged on his ear and rapped on the wall to ward off his wife's dire prediction. "What is this calamity?"

"Your nephew Halil wishes to go into trade," Ayten answered with dark eyes.

"Trade?" Hodja snorted. "That would be folly. Money flows through the boy's fingers like water through a sieve, and his head is as empty as his purse. What fool would sponsor him as a merchant?"

"That is what I am trying to tell you, husband," Ayten said. "I have just come from the marketplace where everyone is saying that Halil is coming here to ask *you* for the money."

Hodja's eyes widened in alarm. "What can he mean by coming to me? Does he think my turban is stuffed with gold liras to squander on his schemes?"

"Halil has always been spoiled," Ayten answered. "You know his mother gives him whatever he asks for."

"And now he is asking us," Hodja said, thoughtfully stroking his beard. "If I refuse Halil, the town gossips will call me a miser. But if I give him the money and his business fails, their wagging tongues will call me a fool for supporting him."

"Misfortune has fallen on our heads," Ayten wailed, wringing her hands. "Better to throw our few coins down the well rather than give them to that wastrel Halil. But what choice do we have? He knows we cannot refuse such a close relative."

Hodja's face cleared at her words. "Ah Ayten! You are as wise as you are beautiful," he said with a grin. "Fear not, I know just what to do *inshallah.*"

A few hours later, Nasreddin Hodja answered a knock at his door and found a smiling Halil waiting at the doorstep. Hodja welcomed him inside and greeted him cordially. "*Hosh geldin,* your visit brings us joy, Nephew."

Halil kissed the back of Hodja's hand and pressed it to his forehead in respect. "*Hosh bulduk,* I have found joy in coming, Uncle."

Ayten served glasses of steaming tea while Hodja waited patiently for his nephew to bring the conversation around to the desired loan. By the time Halil had explained his business plans, Hodja was ready with his answer.

"Of course, my son. I will be glad to help you with the necessary funds as soon as I see that you are ready," Hodja said. Halil's confident grin faltered.

"But Uncle," he asked, "How will you know when I'm ready?"

"I have devised a test," Hodja answered. "Every day without fail, you will throw a gold lira into my well. When you have done this to my satisfaction, I will give you the money you need to start your business."

This seemed a simple request and Halil quickly agreed to Nasreddin Hodja's condition in exchange for the promised loan. The next morning he returned and tossed a coin into the well under Hodja's watchful eye.

"Am I ready yet, Uncle?" Halil asked hopefully.

"Not today," Hodja answered.

Day after day Halil came to throw coins in the well and request the promised loan. Day after day Hodja would answer, "Not today." Soon Halil had used up his few coins and had to borrow money from his mother. And still Hodja answered, "Not today." After a week of this, his mother snapped, "I have no more coins to waste in wells."

Then Halil was forced to beg money from his friends, but they likewise soon tired of giving coins to Halil to throw away. And still Hodja answered, "Not today."

Finally, when he could neither beg nor borrow even one more coin, a desperate Halil hired himself out as a day laborer just to earn money to throw into the well. Every evening he would arrive at Hodja's house sweaty, dirty and exhausted to drop his days pay into the well and ask, "Am I ready *yet*, Uncle?"

And each time Hodja would answer, "Not today."

Then one day, Halil lifted his daily coin over the mouth of the well and hesitated. He stared at the coin for some time before putting it back in his pocket. Then he said to Hodja, "Forgive me, Uncle, but I can no longer throw away what I have earned with such effort."

"Then at last you are ready," Hodja answered with a smile. Hodja reached down into the well and hauled up the fishing net he had hung below the water. It was filled with gold liras. "And here," Hodja said, "is the money I promised. Use it wisely now that you understand its true value."

Although Halil never became rich as a merchant, it is said that he was successful enough to both marry and provide for his mother in her old age, and that is sufficient wealth for any man. May we all share in his good fortune.

> *"The one who asks is shamed once,*
> *but he who refuses a request is shamed twice."*
> —*Turkish Proverb*

Who Do You Believe?

asreddin Hodja was once afflicted by a selfish neighbor who abused whatever he borrowed. If he borrowed a knife, it would return to Hodja dull. If he borrowed a tool, it would be returned damaged. When he borrowed money, it would be repaid only after persistent reminders.

One morning, this neighbor knocked on Nasreddin Hodja's door and said, "*Selamunaleykum*, peace be with you, Hodja. If it is not too much trouble, I would like to borrow your donkey." Hodja saw the man's own donkey limping behind him.

Knowing that his neighbor would return his animal beaten and unfed, Hodja determined on a polite refusal. "*Aleykumselam*, peace be upon you as well," replied Hodja. "I wish that I could be of service. Unfortunately, I have already loaned out my animal to someone else."

But as soon as Hodja made this excuse, his donkey brayed loudly from the stable.

When he heard the animal, the neighbor angrily accused Nasreddin Hodja of lying. "Come now, Hodja, I can hear your donkey right there in the stable."

Hodja wrapped himself in his dignity and answered coolly, "Anyone who believes the word of a donkey above my own does not deserve to be loaned anything." He then slammed the door in his neighbor's face.

"A loan goes out with smiles and returns with tears."
—*Turkish proverb*

The Wondrous Cauldron

 ne day Nasreddin Hodja wished to entertain his friends and went to his neighbor to borrow a large copper cauldron. The next morning, he returned the borrowed cauldron to its owner with his thanks.

"What is this?" asked his neighbor, spying a small coffee pot inside his cauldron.

"May Allah be praised a thousand times. Let me be the first to congratulate you, my friend! Your most excellent cauldron gave birth to that small pot last night," replied the Hodja.

Hodja's neighbor was delighted with this news and accepted both the cauldron and the coffee pot.

When Hodja asked for the loan of the cauldron again, his neighbor readily agreed. This time, however, Nasreddin Hodja did not return the cauldron promptly. In fact, he did not return it at all. When the neighbor could wait no longer, he came knocking on Nasreddin Hodja's door.

"What happened to my cauldron?" he asked. "Why have you not returned it?"

"Have you not heard?" the Hodja asked somberly. "May Allah give you comfort. Your poor cauldron died last week."

"Don't be ridiculous, Hodja," the neighbor answered hotly. "How can a cauldron die?"

"Well, why not?" the Hodja replied. "If you believe that it could give birth, surely you must believe that it could also die?"

One Is More than Two

t has been said that a wise counselor is honored, but the wisest counselor is unnoticed. And so it was when the clever Nasreddin Hodja managed to cloak his advice in such a way as to preserve the domestic happiness of his friend Mehmet.

The sharp-eyed Hodja was the first to notice when the thrifty Mehmet began spending long afternoons at the bazaar instead of at home in his fields. "Wherever the leaf flutters, there is wind," he reasoned. "There must be a reason behind this new habit." And it wasn't long before Hodja discovered that reason in the looks he saw passing between Mehmet and the comely daughter of a certain merchant.

Now Allah had already blessed Mehmet with a lovely and virtuous wife to whom he owed much of his happiness. But Mehmet was the sort of man who looks at his neighbor's scrawny chicken and sees a plump duck and was thus never quite content with his own. Although Mehmet was well able to support a second wife, Nasreddin Hodja felt certain that his friend had not reckoned with the true cost of such an acquisition.

Hodja knew that Mehmet was a proud man unlikely to be turned aside by direct counsel. He also knew that pride can be put to many uses. And so it was that Nasreddin Hodja invited Mehmet to join him for tea one day at a crowded teahouse.

After they had chatted together over hot glasses of *chay* for some time, Hodja leaned back in his chair and said, "How pleasant it is to enjoy the company of a friend! Even so, I would not ruin a man's home to get it as Ahmet did."

"What on earth do you mean, Hodja?" Mehmet asked.

"Surely, you have heard the sad tale of Ahmet and Ali?" Hodja asked in apparent surprise.

Mehmet assured Hodja that he had heard no such story and the other patrons of the teahouse pulled their chairs closer, for one of Nasreddin Hodja's tales was not to be missed. Hodja grinned at his audience and began.

"Ahmet and Ali had been childhood friends so when they met in the bazaar one day they had much to say to another. It was then that Ali learned that Ahmet had taken a second wife.

"'A second wife is a pleasure that every man should know,' Ahmet bragged. 'It is like having a garden on the east and west of your house—when the sun shines too hot on one side, you just refresh yourself in the cool shade of the other. It is like having an orchard where something is always ripe for harvest.'

25

"*Ali became jealous of his friend's happy situation. His wife was an attractive and virtuous woman but why, he wondered, should he not be twice as happy with two wives? Soon after, he took a second wife himself. But when he brought her home, all was not as he had expected.*

"*Ali's new wife wanted nothing to do with him saying, 'I saw the way you looked at your first wife. It is obvious that she is the one you love. Leave me alone.'*

"*Disappointed, Ali returned to his first wife, but she also rejected him saying, 'Why don't you go to your new wife, since I am no longer enough for you?'*

"*Ali went back and forth between the two in this way until they finally threw him out of the house.*

"*Ashamed to admit his situation to his family or friends, Ali wandered in the cold night and finally decided to take refuge in the local mosque. When he entered the darkened building, he saw a figure he at first took for a beggar curled up on the carpet. But when the man rose he realized it was his friend Ahmet!*

"*'Ahmet? What are you doing here in the middle of the night?' Ali asked in surprise.*

"*Ahmet bowed his head sadly. 'I dare not return home. My two wives have made my life so miserable,' he said.*

"*'Why then did you boast to me about the manifold pleasures of a second wife?' Ali demanded angrily.*

"*'Because,' Ahmet admitted sheepishly, 'it has been so lonely here at the mosque.'*"

When Hodja finished his tale, the men in the teahouse roared with laughter. Mehmet, however, just stared down at his tea and said nothing. Soon after, Mehmet rose to leave. Hodja asked him if he would like to meet the following day at the bazaar.

"I do not think I will have business in the bazaar for some time," Mehmet answered quietly. "But you and your wise stories are always welcome in our happy home, my Hodja."

Hodja smiled. Now he was certain that it would remain happy.

"The drum sounds sweeter from a distance."
—Turkish proverb

The Best of Three

ne day, Emperor Tamerlane was troubled that his Turkish subjects seemed to fear him much but love him little. Nasreddin Hodja chanced to be in the court that day, so the Emperor asked him why this was so.

"Your Majesty's commitment to justice has spread like a crimson carpet to the four corners of the world," Hodja answered glancing at the well-stained executioner's block in the courtyard below. "If you would win the hearts of the people, however, you must not only punish evil but reward good. Is not Allah, King Over All Kingdoms, known as both the Judge and the Exalter?"

The Emperor was pleased with this advice and handed Hodja a gold crown. "Perhaps it would be better to crown a head than to chop another off. Now go present this crown to the person who has most ably served his fellow citizens. And be sure that your choice is a popular one," Tamerlane added with a scowl, "or I may decide that the block is best after all."

Hodja immediately wished he had kept his counsel to himself. He realized that finding a virtuous citizen was one thing, but getting all the people to agree on a single candidate was another. Nevertheless Hodja kept his doubts to himself. "To hear is to obey," he said with a bow and left to make the necessary preparations.

Soon he had narrowed the field of contenders down to a final three: a poet, an artist, and a doctor, each of whom had great popular support. A large group gathered at the palace to see which of the three would receive the golden crown.

The poet went first and recited his best-known poem, which made the crowd sigh with pleasure. While Hodja was listening to the poem, his glance fell on an old woman at the front of the crowd. When the poet finished, she smiled brightly, cheered loudly, and clapped her hands as if to say, "This is the one who deserves the crown."

Then it was the artist's turn. He displayed some of the beautiful artwork that had graced the local mosque and other locations in the city. While the crowd marveled over the artist's creations, Hodja watched the old woman for her reaction.

To his surprise, she again smiled brightly, cheered loudly, and clapped her hands as if to say, "This is the one who deserves the crown." As for Hodja, he couldn't choose between the two.

The third contender was a doctor, who had discovered the cure to a recent plague. Hodja kept his eyes on the old woman. Again she smiled brightly, cheered loudly and clapped her hands as if to say, "This is the one who deserves the crown."

Hodja could not choose a clear victor from the three worthy candidates. The crowd seemed divided in their support with large groups favoring the poet, the artist, and the doctor for the prize. Unable to come to a decision, Nasreddin Hodja called the woman forward to seek her opinion.

"My aunt," he said as he kissed her hand and touched it to his forehead in respect. "You alone seem to support all three candidates. Can you not assist me in choosing between them?"

The woman shyly answered, "Allah forbid that I should do such a thing, Hodja effendi. The three men who stand before you today are all my sons, and I am here only to support them and see who will win. Far be it from me to choose one above another and so stir up jealousy between them."

When Hodja heard this, he smiled broadly. At last he had the answer he sought. Hodja motioned the crowd for silence and lifted the crown high for all to see. "My countrymen, how shall we choose between such wonders? Our poet has delighted our ears, our artist has enchanted our eyes, and our doctor has preserved our very lives. Yet there is another among us who has surpassed all three."

Then Hodja drew the mother of the three men forward and placed the crown on her head saying, "This woman has raised all three to be a treasure to us all. Shall we not honor her who stands behind these great men?"

Then the crowd roared their approval in unison, with the three sons smiling brightly, cheering loudly, and clapping their hands shouting, "Here is the one who deserves the crown!"

Not Too Deeply

nce Nasreddin Hodja traveled to Konya where he required the signature of a certain kadi in order to complete his business. When he brought his papers to court, the kadi said that he did not have time to sign it just then. When Hodja appeared at court on the following day, however, the clerk told him that the kadi was still too busy and that he should return again on the next day. After several days of such treatment, Nasreddin Hodja realized that the kadi was stalling him in expectation of a bribe.

Nasreddin Hodja was angered by the kadi's greed and determined to teach the corrupt official a lesson while acquiring the necessary signature. He took a large jar and filled it most of the way with ox dung. Hodja then covered the dung with a layer of honey. Taking this jar to the court, he presented it to the kadi with his compliments. At once, the kadi found time to sign his documents.

After Nasreddin Hodja had the signature safely in his hands, he asked, "Kadi effendi, aren't you ashamed of taking that jar of honey?"

The kadi smirked at him and said, "My friend, let us not go too deeply into that." Then the judge scooped some honey from the top of the jar and licked his finger with satisfaction. "What delicious honey this is."

"Well, as you said, let us not go too deeply into that," answered Hodja and quickly left the court to complete his business and return home to Akshehir.

Inshallah

asreddin Hodja studied the night sky through his bedroom window. "What sort of weather do you suppose we'll see tomorrow, Ayten?" he asked his wife.

"Allah alone knows, husband," Ayten answered as she busied herself with rolling out their sleeping mattresses for the night. "But there will be plenty of work to do in any case. If it rains, I shall weave *inshallah*, if God wills. If the sun shines, I shall go to the river and wash the clothes *inshallah.*"

"If the weather is fine tomorrow, I'm going to the fields to plow," announced Hodja.

Ayten looked at her husband darkly. "Do not forget to say '*inshallah*' husband."

Nasreddin Hodja ignored his wife's advice and continued, "If it rains tomorrow, I will go to the hills to chop wood."

"Remember your humility, husband," Ayten warned again. "Do not presume to plan anything without adding '*inshallah.*'"

But Ayten's gentle correction was like dry leaves on the fire of Hodja's stubbornness. "Why should I when my course is certain?" he said defiantly as he climbed into bed. "Either it will rain or it will not rain, and I have decided what to do in either case."

Ayten pursed her lips, tugged her ear and knocked on the wall to ward off the bad luck that was certain to follow Hodja's impious course. But she was far too wise to argue with an obstinate husband, so she blew out the poppy oil lamp and felt her way to the mattress. Poor Ayten tossed and turned in her sleep, but Nasreddin passed the night in peaceful snores.

In the morning, there was a steady patter of raindrops and the darkened sky threatened more to come.

"This day I weave *inshallah*," said Ayten. She sat down to a quiet day at her loom, weaving a new cotton shirt for her stubborn husband.

"Today I chop wood," said Nasreddin Hodja. Not all of Ayten's pleading could persuade him to utter a single "*inshallah.*"

Hodja lifted his ax over his shoulder and went to the stable to harness his donkey for the journey to the woods. Then he found that his donkey had gone lame overnight.

At first, Hodja was relieved. The donkey's lameness and the miserable weather were perfect excuses for a quiet day at home. He started back toward the house, humming happily to himself. Then Hodja stopped. How could he face Ayten if he failed to go to the hills to chop wood today? She was certain to point out that the donkey's lameness was Allah's judgment on him for failing to say *"inshallah."* He decided that he would rather endure the rain than Ayten's triumph.

Hodja reluctantly shambled out onto the road. He walked along slowly through the growing puddles, wishing that some sympathetic friend would come along and persuade him that he should not be out in such weather.

His heart jumped when he saw a group of men at the crossroads ahead. Surely one of them would say, "Poor Hodja effendi! What are you doing on foot in this rain?" and convince him to go home for a glass of hot tea. But as he came closer, he saw that the men were soldiers. Hodja did not like the way they were watching him, but it was too late to turn back.

"Here, old man!" One of the soldiers stepped directly in front of Nasreddin Hodja. "Show us the way to Karabash!"

"Karabash?" Nasreddin Hodja shrugged, trying his best to appear too senile to know the way. "Karabash?" A journey to the hills for wood was a short stroll compared to the long, winding road to Karabash. "Karabash?"

"You won't fool us so easily!" The soldiers began beating Hodja with sticks. They shook him. They pounded him. They slapped him.

"I remember the way now!" shouted Hodja from under the rain of blows.

"Good, then you can lead us there," the captain told him. "March!"

Nasreddin Hodja cast a wistful glance at the hills, where he could have spent the day in the shelter of the woods, swinging his ax a bit now and then. Then he looked back toward his own home where Ayten was no doubt sitting by the fire weaving contentedly.

Hodja turned dejectedly toward the path to Karabash. The mud sucked greedily at his boots with each step. The rain slapped at his face. Whenever he stopped to catch his breath or to shake the mud from his feet, a grim soldier would prod him into motion again. As he trudged wearily onward, he thought of Ayten, the wise Ayten who had said, "I shall weave *inshallah,*" and was now sitting snugly before her loom. On and on he plodded.

It was nearly dusk by the time Hodja had delivered the soldiers to the gates of Karabash and turned wearily back toward home. He pushed himself to make as much of the journey as possible while a glimmer of daylight lasted. Soon it was so dark that he was often obliged to grope on his knees in the mud to find the road. Again he thought of Ayten in her dry cozy house, the wise Ayten who had said, "I shall weave, *inshallah*." On and on he plodded.

It was midnight when Nasreddin Hodja at last stumbled over the welcome cobblestones of the streets of Akshehir. His feet were blistered, and his robe soaked through and heavy with mud as he staggered at last through his own gate. Exhausted, he leaned against his front door and jangled the knocker to awaken the sleeping Ayten.

"Who is there?" she called anxiously from within.

"Oh, Ayten," answered Nasreddin Hodja in a cautious voice. "It is I, your great fool of a husband *inshallah*."

The Wrong Cow

asreddin Hodja was so generous with his hospitality and wise counsel that he had earned the love and goodwill of all the people of Akshehir. Almost all.

One of his neighbors, the local kadi, was jealous of Hodja's excellent reputation and always found fault with him. If Hodja entertained friends in the evening, the kadi complained that their noise kept him awake. If Hodja and his guests kept quiet, the kadi would demand to know why they kept such suspicious secrecy. Hodja bore these complaints with unfailing patience, which only infuriated the kadi more.

One day, the kadi made an appointment with Nasreddin Hodja to discuss certain new complaints, which he had lately discovered. But when the kadi arrived at the appointed hour, he found his neighbor away from home. Hodja had forgotten their appointment while drinking tea with a friend in the marketplace.

The kadi paced in front of Hodja's door for some time in mounting frustration. Finally, he picked up a piece of charcoal and wrote "Arrogant Donkey" on Hodja's door. Then he stomped off to the teahouse to gossip about this latest offense.

When Nasreddin Hodja returned home and saw the writing, he hurried to the teahouse where he found the kadi complaining loudly about him.

"Please forgive me for not being home to welcome you," Hodja said humbly, "I had forgotten our appointment. Of course, I remembered as soon as I saw that you had left your name at my door."

The kadi's face reddened dangerously as the men at the teahouse erupted in laughter. As the kadi stomped back to his courtroom, Hodja reflected that he would do well to stay clear of any legal entanglements in the future. Unfortunately, a different fate was written on his forehead. The kadi's cow and Hodja's cow had disputes of their own, and one day Hodja was compelled to visit the kadi in his courtroom.

When the kadi saw Nasreddin Hodja in his packed court, he was delighted at the opportunity to humiliate Hodja publicly. "What have you done, Hodja?" the kadi demanded. "Whatever your offense, be sure that you will pay for it in full."

"Kadi effendi, I have come to you for justice," Hodja said sorrowfully. "Our cows have been fighting again, and your cow has killed mine. I wish to know what the penalty is for a murderous cow."

The kadi had no intention of penalizing his own cow but made a show of consulting his law books. "The law states that a dumb animal cannot be held responsible for its actions in such a case," the kadi said. "The cow cannot be penalized."

"But Kadi effendi," Hodja exclaimed, "Surely the owner of the cow must be held responsible and pay some compensation for the lost animal."

"The owner in such a case cannot be held responsible either, Hodja," the kadi insisted.

"Kadi effendi, are you quite certain that neither the cow nor its owner can be punished in any way?" Hodja asked again.

"Yes, Hodja," the kadi said spitefully, "I am entirely certain."

"I see. Thank you for explaining the matter so clearly before Allah and these witnesses," Hodja answered with a smile. "Unfortunately, in my distress I may have misspoke earlier. You see, it was *my* cow that killed *yours.*"

"Sharp vinegar damages its own container."
(A bad temper harms its possessor)
—Turkish proverb

Hodja's Threat

nce there was and twice there wasn't a day when Nasreddin Hodja was traveling along the famed Silk Road while serving at the court of the terrible conqueror Tamerlane. Along the way, he spent the night at a caravansaray and refreshed himself from the rigors of travel with a hot meal and soft bed. In the morning, however, he discovered that his precious donkey had been stolen from the stables.

The innkeepers disclaimed any responsibility, saying, "Each must look to his own, Hodja, if he would not suffer loss in these hard times." Hodja's fellow travelers likewise claimed no knowledge of the theft.

Enraged by their apathy, Hodja called out in a loud voice to all of them, saying, "Listen well, countrymen! If my lost donkey is not returned within the hour, be sure that I will do just as my mighty master Tamerlane did when his horse was stolen! I have nothing more to say on this matter."

While his threat hung in the air, Hodja sat down to breakfast. The other travelers became alarmed when they discovered that Hodja was connected to the tyrant Tamerlane. Fearing for their heads, they scoured the surrounding area in search of the missing donkey.

And so it was that Hodja's donkey was soon returned to the stable where it was well fed, groomed, and loaded down with extra provisions by the anxious stablehands. At the appointed hour, a satisfied Hodja entered the stable and prepared to resume his journey.

The young stable boy who attended Hodja was bursting with curiosity and finally asked, "Please Hodja effendi, what would you have done had your donkey not been returned?"

Nasreddin Hodja grinned and answered, "I, like the great Tamerlane, would have taken my saddlebags on my back and walked."

The Fairness of Allah

nce there was and twice there wasn't a wealthy merchant who wished to earn a little *sevap*, favor with God, in order to balance the scales after some of his sharper dealings at the marketplace. The merchant reached into his handsome silk robes and tossed a small sack of coins to a group of beggar boys in the town square.

The boys scrambled after the coins, calling out blessings toward the merchant, "*Allah kabul etsin*, may God accept your piety!" It wasn't long, however, before they began fighting with one another over how to share the coins. Just then, Nasreddin Hodja happened by and pulled them apart.

"For the love of Allah," Hodja scolded. "Why are you behaving in this shameless manner?"

Knowing Hodja's wise reputation, the boys explained their dispute and asked him to resolve the matter by dividing the coins between them fairly.

"Very well, boys," Nasreddin Hodja answered with a twinkle in his eye. "But answer me this first: do you wish me to judge according to the fairness of Man or the fairness of Allah?"

"We want you to judge according to the fairness of Allah," the boys answered.

Hodja reached into the sack of coins and gave a handful of coins to the first boy. To the second boy, he gave five coins. To the third boy he gave three coins. To a fourth boy he gave one coin. The other boys received nothing.

The empty-handed boys protested loudly saying, "Hodja, we asked you to divide these fairly!"

"And so I have," Hodja answered. "If you had asked for Man's fairness, I would have divided the coins evenly among you, for that is what men call fairness. But you asked for the fairness of Allah. Have you not seen that God portions his blessings unequally, giving much to some and little or nothing to others?"

The boys looked down at their own tattered clothes. Then they remembered the smooth silks of the merchant, and they admitted the truth of Hodja's words.

"Then be not too quick to cry out for God's fairness," Hodja said. "For Allah alone knows what that will be."

Thus it was that Nasreddin Hodja left the boys, some richer, but all of them wiser. May we all share in their good fortune.

Animal Years

henever Emperor Tamerlane became bored with the flattery of his court, he found relief in the companionship of Nasreddin Hodja. Hodja's good-natured honesty was like a cool rain in summer to Tamerlane who appreciated his humorous insights.

One day, Tamerlane asked Hodja to sit beside his golden throne while he took counsel and granted audience to his many servants and officials. He hoped Hodja would enliven this dull task with his shrewd remarks.

A young officer stepped forward to report his capture of some local bandits. When the officer marched crisply away, the Emperor smiled approvingly. "Did you see the fire in his eyes, Hodja? If only all my soldiers were so zealous in their duties."

"Of course, my lord," Hodja replied. "What else would one expect from a dog?"

The Emperor frowned. What did Hodja mean by comparing that estimable soldier to a dog? Did he know something that Tamerlane did not? But he had no time to question Nasreddin Hodja as the royal architect was already advancing to report on the progress of the Emperor's latest building project.

Tamerlane couldn't help noticing how weary the architect looked. Though his beard was not yet white, he seemed stooped beneath the weight of his turban. After the architect bowed to the Emperor and retreated from the throne room, Tamerlane remarked, "How burdened he looks. You would think he was carrying the new mosque on his back instead of designing it."

"Of course, my lord," Hodja replied. "What else would one expect from a donkey?"

The Emperor scowled darkly. How could Hodja compare his valued servant to a donkey? But before he could admonish Hodja to mind his tongue, Tamerlane's clouded face broke into a sunny smile as his littlest grandson toddled through the splendid brass doors of the throne room. At the sight of the Emperor, the boy shrieked with delight and threw himself into Tamerlane's outstretched arms.

The greatest men of the empire affected patience outside while the boy giggled at his grandfather's funny faces and bounced on his knee. By the time his grandson was returned to his nursemaid, Tamerlane was in a splendid mood. "Ah Hodja," Tamerlane said with a grin, "how is it that I, the mightiest of men, can take such pleasure in the smiles of a child?"

"But of course, my lord," Hodja replied. "What else would one expect

37

from a monkey?"

Tamerlane's face purpled with rage as he reached for the knife at his belt. "You presume too much, Hodja! It is one thing to insult my servants, but the tongue that wags too far will be cut out."

"I had thought my lord might take some small pleasure in my observations," Hodja answered mildly. "Can it be that you have never heard the tale of 'Adam and the Animal Years'?"

"Indeed I have not," Tamerlane said, now curious. "Perhaps your tongue can wag its way out of trouble by enlightening me."

Nasreddin Hodja smiled and began.

"At the beginning of all things, when the earth was as fresh as new skimmed cream, Allah made all creatures as he saw fit. Allah first created the Dog, saying 'Your name is Dog. You shall have a lifespan of twenty-five years. Live as a dog.'

"But the first Dog pleaded with Allah saying, 'My Lord, twenty-five years will be too much for me. I shall be worn out from chasing everything that catches my eye and marking my territory. Please let my lot be reduced to fifteen years.'

"And Allah in his mercy granted the Dog's wish and shortened his life to fifteen years.

"Next Allah created the Donkey, saying 'Your name is Donkey. You shall have forty years. Live as a donkey.'

"But the Donkey pleaded with Allah saying, 'My lord, forty years will be too much for me. I shall be worn out from carrying heavy burdens and the crack of the whip. Please let my lot be reduced to twenty years.'

"And Allah in his mercy granted the Donkey's wish.

"Next Allah created the Monkey saying, 'Your name is Monkey. You shall have fifty years. Live as a monkey.'

"But the Monkey also pleaded with Allah saying, 'Fifty years will be too much for me. I shall be worn out from leaping about and playing the fool. Please let my lot be reduced to thirty years.'

"And Allah in his mercy granted the Monkey's wish.

"At last, Allah created man saying, 'Your name is Man. You shall have twenty years. Live as a human being.'

"But the Man was unhappy with his portion and pleaded with God for more life saying, 'Twenty years are too few for your steward on earth, the crown of your creation. Please allow me to have the years that the Dog, the Donkey, and the Monkey did not want, for why should they go to waste?'

"Then Allah laughed and accepted the man's bold request saying, 'Very well, I shall add the years of the Dog, the Donkey, and the Monkey to your own. May you find contentment in them.'

"It is for this reason that men live the first twenty years of their lives as a human being, surrounded by the love of their family, their every need provided for as Allah intended. But after this blessed time, the Dog years begin when a man must run hard for ten years after his desires, scratch out a living, and mark out a place for himself in the world. After that, he must bear the heavy weight of responsibility like a Donkey for twenty years as he raises his children and provides for his growing household. Finally, a man enters his Monkey years when he makes all manner of silly faces and plays the fool to amuse his grandchildren."

"So you see, my lord," Hodja concluded, "it is our common lot to live as Man, Dog, Donkey, and Monkey as our first ancestor requested. Whether or not he was wise to ask such a thing some may wonder, but the animal years are not without their pleasures—the thrill of the chase, the satisfaction of bearing up under a heavy load, and the joy of a laughing grandchild. For my part, I am content."

Then Tamerlane considered Hodja's words. He remembered his own ambitious youth, the heavy labors of building an empire, and the delight of his grandson's visit and forgot all his anger when he saw that Hodja had indeed spoken wisely. It is said that Emperor Tamerlane grew into a wiser judge of men from that day on. May we all share in his good fortune.

The Tin Whistle

t seems strange that the heart should be captivated by a mere sound: a miser by the clink of coins, a mother by the coo of her child, and a boy by the note of a tin whistle. But so it was in the city of Akshehir when the muhtar's son returned one day from the bazaar with a shiny new whistle. Soon every boy was determined to gain such a prize for himself.

When the boys saw Nasreddin Hodja saddling his donkey to make the journey to the bazaar, they swarmed around him like bees to the flower.

"In the name of Allah the Compassionate and Merciful, will you not bring me a whistle, Hodja effendi?"

"Hodja effendi, you are as generous as you are wise. Surely you will not begrudge me a whistle."

"Hodja, my heart will break if you do not bring me a whistle also."

With such words, they begged and flattered and pleaded with Hodja to buy tin whistles for them all at the bazaar. All except one boy who pushed his way through the crowd and pressed a few small coins into Nasreddin Hodja's palm and said, "I would like a whistle please."

When Hodja returned in the evening, the boys rushed out to meet him. Hodja removed a whistle from his pocket and handed it to the boy who had given him the coins. As the boy blew his whistle happily, the other boys crowded forward eagerly with their hands outstretched until Hodja turned out his pockets to show that he had no more whistles.

Some of the boys began to cry and complain, but Hodja silenced them with a rebuke. "It takes more than importunate words to acquire your heart's desire, boys. In this world, the one who pays plays the whistle."

This tale is so well known in Turkey that it has become a proverb. When someone asks for what they have not earned, they may be reminded, "The one who pays plays the whistle."

Hodja's Knife

A day came when the conqueror Tamerlane feared a popular rebellion and determined to disarm the Turkish population so that they could not rise against him. His advisors counseled against this, arguing that the Turks were a proud people. They worried that such a measure would spark the very uprising that the Emperor sought to prevent.

As stubborn as he was proud, Tamerlane would not be dissuaded. He had a decree written and posted throughout the city that any Turk found bearing arms would be put to death.

The next day, Nasreddin Hodja was found carrying a large knife. Tamerlane's soldiers seized Hodja and brought him before the Emperor.

"You know that I have issued a decree forbidding weapons, Hodja," said Tamerlane angrily. "Do you mean to defy my authority by carrying a blade openly on the streets?"

"May Allah forbid any such thought, my lord," Hodja answered. "I assure you that this is no weapon but merely an instrument of truth. When I come across a dangerous error in a bit of writing, I use a knife to cut it out."

"Are you mocking me, Hodja?" Tamerlane asked as his eyes narrowed dangerously. "Do you expect me to believe that you need such a large knife just to cut out errors?"

"I assure you, my lord," Hodja answered softly, "some errors are so great that even as large a blade as this would be too small for their removal."

Tamerlane sat in silence for some time before dismissing Hodja.

The following day the decree was lifted.

What About the Thieves?

 ne evening Nasreddin Hodja and his wife Ayten returned from visiting friends to discover that their house had been robbed.

"This is all your fault, Nasreddin," scolded his wife. "You should have checked that the house was locked securely before we left!"

Awakened by the cries of his wife, Hodja's neighbors rushed over. Embarrassed that the theft had occurred under their noses, they were also quick to find fault with Hodja, saying:

"You should have left a lamp burning in your house to discourage thieves."

"Why did you not hang a blue bead over the door to ward off bad luck?"

"I always urged you to get a watchdog."

Hodja raised his hand to interrupt them with a proverb: *"After the wagon overturns, many come forward to show the correct road.* But surely I am not the *only* one to blame?"

"Oh? And who else should we blame?" they all asked.

"Well, what about the thieves?"

Not My Equal

asreddin Hodja was generous with his advice, but his own affairs were often neglected while he assisted others. As a result, he was richly honored but poorly financed. When his purse was as empty as a beggar's belly, he would sometimes travel through the countryside collecting the donations that faithful Muslims give to those who have devoted their lives to the study of the holy Koran.

One day, on just such a journey, he arrived in a town far from home and was invited to spend the night with a wealthy merchant there. Over dinner, the merchant expressed his delight in the Koran. Nasreddin Hodja smiled broadly, hoping for a generous donation from this professed admirer of the blessed Prophet.

In the morning, Nasreddin Hodja politely asked his host for a donation. In reply, the merchant requested that Hodja read him a passage from the Koran in Arabic. Hodja read the passage fluently with just the right intonations, but the man was not impressed. He picked up the Koran and read the same passage just as well as Hodja did. Next the man asked Hodja to write out a few verses. He did so, and then the host also wrote down the same verses neatly and accurately.

Then the merchant said to Hodja, "Now you see that I know the Koran just as well as you. You came to ask me for a donation, but why should I give it? I am your equal and have no need of you."

"Well, you can read and write Arabic," replied Hodja, "but we are not equal."

"Oh?" said the merchant haughtily. "Why is that?"

Hodja replied, "When you have learned that the Koran is more than Arabic, that generosity is more than personal need, and that pride is more than humiliating others, *then* you will be my equal."

The Wisdom of Pumpkins

One day Nasreddin Hodja was traveling and turned aside from the road to cool off beneath the shade of a walnut tree. As he rested, Hodja reflected on his many worries and troubles. Soon he found himself, as men often do at such times, questioning the wisdom and goodness of Allah.

"If I were Almighty Allah," he mused, "I would arrange the world differently." Then he noticed a line of pumpkins growing in a nearby garden. "Here is one thing I'm certain I could improve upon. Why should that huge pumpkin grow on a slender little vine, while the little walnut grows upon a mighty tree that is strong enough to hold a donkey. It is a senseless match. Were I lord of creation, I would have put the little walnut on that puny vine and the great pumpkin on this powerful tree."

Just then Hodja felt a painful *shak!* on his bald head as a walnut fell from the tree. Hodja gave a cry and massaged the top of his head where a bump was beginning to swell. Then a smile slowly crossed his face, and he raised his hands to the sky in supplication.

"Oh Allah, who sees me and knows me, small as I am!" he exclaimed. "With what wisdom did you put walnuts on this tree. Had I arranged matters, my head would have been crushed by a pumpkin just now. Great indeed is thy goodness and mercy. From now on, I shall trust the ordering of the universe to you."

"One who loves roses will endure thorns."
——Turkish proverb

The Lost Ring

ne day Nasreddin Hodja's neighbor came to visit and found Hodja on his hands and knees in the garden, peering intently at the ground.

"What are you doing, Hodja?" his neighbor asked.

Hodja replied, "I have lost my gold ring and I am trying to find it."

"A gold ring?" exclaimed the man. "Let me help you search for it."

Another neighbor passed by and noticed the two men crawling in the dirt. "*Kolay gelsin*, may it come easily. What are you two doing?" she asked curiously.

The man replied, "We are searching for Hodja's lost ring."

"Poor Hodja!" exclaimed the woman. "Let me help you search for the ring too. A woman's eyes are sharper than a falcon's."

Then a group of children walked by and saw the three crawling around in the dirt. The eldest boy asked, "Why are you crawling on the ground?"

The woman replied, "We are searching for Hodja's lost ring. Why don't you make yourselves useful and help us look."

The children swarmed through the small garden searching for the ring. Finally, after some time, a young boy asked Nasreddin Hodja, "Hodja effendi, are you certain that you dropped your ring out here?"

"Oh no," Hodja replied, "I lost the ring somewhere inside my house."

"Then why are we all looking for it outside?" the boy asked.

"I already tried that, but it was too dark inside to find anything," Hodja explained. "The light is much better out here."

The Wise Answer

asreddin Hodja had a full turban but a flat purse and the day finally came when his creditors emptied his house to settle his debts. *"A loan comes with smiles and departs with tears,"* said Hodja sadly, and the weight of his loss bowed his head to the floor in sorrow.

But Allah smiles on faithful heart and ready tongue and so it was with Hodja. At that moment, a delegation from a distant town arrived in search of a new imam for their mosque. They had heard of Hodja's deep wisdom but not his shallow resources, so they were surprised when they saw him through the window in an empty room apparently bowed down in prayer. "He must be a very pious man indeed," they all decided.

When they knocked at the door, Nasreddin Hodja graciously greeted them and ushered them inside. The men looked around the bare room and, finding no furniture, sat down on the floor. "Hodja effendi, where is your furniture?" their leader asked curiously.

Unwilling to expose his true situation, Nasreddin Hodja stalled for time. "Where is your furniture?" he asked.

"But Hodja effendi," the man replied, "we don't have any furniture here. We are travelers passing through."

"Exactly," Hodja responded with dignity, "and so am I." Then he politely excused himself to borrow some refreshment for his guests from the neighbors.

The delegation turned to one another and discussed Hodja's words. "He means that we are all travellers in this world on our way to the next," said one.

"That must be why he does not burden himself with material possessions," suggested another.

"Where else can we find such an unworldly saint to serve as our spiritual leader?" their leader asked.

When Hodja returned with tea, the men threw themselves at his feet and begged him to come and be their imam. And so it was that a wise answer turned his loss into gain.

The Bear Hunt

ne day Nasreddin Hodja was walking through the forest when he heard a fierce buzzing. Looking up, he saw a fine-looking beehive hanging on a branch high above. Hodja relished the taste of wild honey, so he began looking for a long branch with which to reach the hive.

Suddenly, he heard the sound of something large crashing through the underbrush. Crackle! Crunch! Snap! It grew steadily louder and nearer. Hodja trembled with fear. This was no rabbit or fox but something far bigger.

Nasreddin Hodja glimpsed a towering mound of black fur approaching. Then he saw a shiny black nose between great dark eyes. It was the largest bear Hodja had ever seen.

"Allah gave man arms to fight but legs to run away," Hodja said to himself, "and a man's legs are longer than his arms!" Hodja scrambled up the beehive tree to escape.

Crackle! Crunch! Snap! The enormous bear plodded out into the open beneath Hodja's hiding place. The brawny bear paid no attention to Hodja but sniffed hungrily toward the beehive. Then, to Hodja's horror, it stuck its powerful claws into the tree and began climbing up.

"Perhaps he won't notice me," Hodja hoped as he clung to the tree trunk, concealed among the leaves. The bear followed its snuffling nose higher and higher toward the beehive until Hodja could feel its hot breath at his feet. Hodja dared not breathe as the bear stopped just beneath him and stretched out a heavy paw toward the hanging beehive and the sticky sweetness within.

As the bear scratched for honey, angry bees began to swarm out of the hive. The bees buzzed around both the bear and Hodja until the poor man could no longer contain himself. Hodja began flailing his arm and shouting at the bees "Peace be upon you, little yellow brothers! Do not punish the innocent alongside this great furry thief! I didn't touch your honey!"

Now the bear was a gentle and shy creature, and wholly unprepared for such loud and sudden screams. With a howl, the bear lost its balance and crashed down through the branches. There was a heavy thud as it hit the ground. Then silence.

The bees now forgotten, Hodja edged warily down the tree. His eyes were fixed on the black heap that lay motionless below him. After each movement, Hodja would wait, watch and listen to be sure that the bear had not moved. By the time he had reached the ground, even the cautious

Hodja was certain that the bear would never frighten anyone again.

Nasreddin Hodja rubbed his weary arms and legs as he started toward home, thinking of the story he would have to tell his wife Ayten over supper. However, the more he imagined telling his frightening tale, the more he felt there would not be much glory in the telling. Something was wrong with a story that featured such a shaky hero.

Suddenly a bright grin shone on Hodja's clouded face. He ran back to the tree, pulled out his knife, and skinned the bear. Then he wrapped the great black pelt over his shoulders and walked out of the forest to Akshehir.

Hodja did not take the shortest path through the city to his house. Instead, he wandered through the busiest streets until all Akshehir was talking about the brave and skillful Hodja who had single-handedly killed a gigantic black bear.

Hodja reveled in his newfound reputation until Emperor Tamerlane arrived at his door one morning with a hunting party. It was then that he discovered that a reputation can be an awkward thing to live up to.

"Saddle your horse, Hodja," Tamerlane said. "I am hunting for bear today, and all Akshehir knows that you are the greatest bear hunter in the land."

"My lord, your party is so large already and too many hunters might frighten away your quarry," Hodja said, thinking quickly. "Perhaps I should not come."

Emperor Tamerlane's eyes narrowed. "I can see what worries you, Hodja."

"You can?" Hodja gulped.

"Of course I can," Tamerlane answered. "You fear that, with so many hunters, you may lose the honor of the kill to another. Fear not. I have given orders that the first bear we find is to be yours alone."

"My Master is the soul of generosity," Hodja answered in a small voice. Finding nothing else to say, he said farewell to his beloved Ayten and rode off with the hunting party.

The sun was red on the horizon by the time Hodja returned.

"Welcome home, my brave hunter!" Ayten cried. She ushered Hodja to his chair, pressed a glass of hot tea into his hand, and sat beside him eagerly to hear the tale that all their neighbors, indeed the whole city, would be asking for tomorrow. The smile on her husband's face promised the best of news, but for once, Hodja said nothing and merely sipped his tea contentedly.

Finally Ayten asked, "How did the hunt go?"

"Wonderful!" Hodja replied.

"How many bears did you kill, husband?" Ayten asked eagerly.

"None."

"Well then, how many did you chase?"

"None."

"Well then, how many did you see?"

"None at all."

"I don't understand, Hodja," his wife persisted. "How can you say the hunt was wonderful when you found no bears?"

"My dear," Hodja replied, "when it comes to hunting bears, none is all you want to find.

Wonderful Religion

ne day Nasreddin Hodja was forced to travel on the road to Sivrihisar during the fast of Ramazan. Along the way, he became faint from thirst, and a friendly farmer invited Hodja to sit beneath his shady tree.

"The blessed prophet excused travelers from the fast," said the farmer. "Please accept my hospitality and refresh yourself before you continue your journey."

Hodja was weary from walking and gladly accepted a cool seat and a plate of bread and olives from the poor farmer. Wishing to repay the man's generosity, Nasreddin Hodja opened a bottle of raki from his pack and offered a glass of the strong liquor to the farmer. Out of politeness, the farmer took a swallow of raki. But once he had taken a swallow, he wanted another and invited Hodja to join him. Soon they were drinking quite freely together.

Now the kadi of the village was a pious man and had forbidden the drinking of alcohol. When he heard that two men were getting drunk in the middle of Ramazan, he was outraged. The kadi decided to make an example of them both and had Hodja and his new friend arrested and dragged into his courtroom.

The kadi turned to the farmer first. "You shameless dog! How could you do such a disgraceful thing on this blessed day? We will see if you like the inside of prison as well as the inside of a bottle!"

The farmer hung his head in disgrace and said nothing.

Then the angry kadi turned his attention to Nasreddin Hodja. "And you, you wretched drunkard! What do you have to say for yourself?"

Thinking quickly, Nasreddin Hodja answered, "Please kadi effendi, I am a Christian."

"You are not one of the faithful," the kadi answered. "Your customs are different from ours with neither prayers nor fasts. It may not be a sin for you to drink raki." Then the kadi ordered that Nasreddin Hodja be released and the farmer taken to prison. But before the farmer could be taken away, Hodja spoke up.

"Kadi effendi," he asked, "would you like to convert an unbeliever to Islam?"

"Of course I would," said the kadi with interest.

"Then I should like to become a Muslim," said Nasreddin Hodja. "But on one condition: you must set my friend here free."

The kadi considered Hodja's proposal and decided that converting an infidel was a more meritorious act than punishing a sinner. He had Hodja repeat the confession of faith, "There is no God but God and Mohammed is his prophet," and then allowed them both to leave.

As they were walking away, Nasreddin Hodja said, "How wonderful religion can be!"

The farmer, who was thinking just the opposite, turned to Hodja in shock and asked, "How can you say that?"

"Well, first I was able to save myself by becoming a Christian," explained Hodja. "Then I became a Muslim and saved you."

The Just Judgment

nce there was and twice there wasn't a time when Nasreddin Hodja served as a kadi and delighted the people of Akshesir with his clear insight and fair judgments. One day a poor widow approached Hodja at court to beg his help with a perplexing problem.

"Your Honor," she said, "I am a widow with no husband to help me raise my son. The boy is addicted to sugar and squanders our few coins on sweets, although we have barely enough to eat. There seems to be nothing I can do or say to cure him of this unhealthy and costly habit. I am here to ask you to forbid him to eat sweets, for I know he will respect your authority."

Nasreddin Hodja stroked his beard thoughtfully as he contemplated the widow's request. "I must give this problem thorough consideration," he replied. "Please come back in a week's time and *inshallah*, God willing, I will have a judgment for you."

A week later, the widow again placed her name upon the list of petitioners and waited her turn. She led her son to the head of the court when her name was called. "I am ready for your pronouncement, Your Honor, and I have brought my son so that he may hear it from your own lips."

Nasreddin Hodja looked at mother and son and slowly shook his head from side to side. "I am truly sorry," Hodja answered. "This is a difficult case. I must postpone my judgment for another week."

Confused but still hopeful, the widow returned home with her son. A week later, and then again the week after that, the widow received the same response from Hodja. Nevertheless she patiently persisted. Finally, a month after her first visit, the widow stood before Nasreddin Hodja and asked again, "Do you have a judgment for my son today?"

Nasreddin Hodja leaned forward in his chair and fixed his eyes on the widow's son. "Boy!" shouted Hodja. "By the authority of this court, you are hereby forbidden to eat sweets!"

The boy cowered before Nasreddin Hodja and meekly bowed his assent. The widow smiled brightly, knowing her problem had been solved. She kissed the back of Hodja's hand, and thanked him for his help. Then she asked the question which had been troubling her for weeks.

"Hodja," she said, "why did you not make that pronouncement weeks ago when I first came to you? Why did you wait so long?"

Nasreddin Hodja looked surprised and answered, "Before I could judge another, I had to cure myself of the same habit. How could I know it would take so long for me to give up sweets?"

Hodja and the Scorpion

ne day Nasreddin Hodja and a friend were sitting beside a river. As they watched the water glide by, a scorpion making its way along the riverbank tumbled into the water and began to struggle and drown. Without hesitation, Hodja reached in and plucked the scorpion from the water. As he placed it safely on the riverbank, the scorpion stung Hodja's hand.

A few minutes later, the same scorpion slipped into the river again. Once more, Hodja rescued it from the water and again it stung his hand.

A little later, the scorpion fell into the water again, and Hodja pulled it out and again it stung his hand.

Unable to restrain himself any longer, the friend cried out, "Hodja! Why do you continue to save that wretched scorpion from drowning? Can't you see that it is just going to sting you again?"

"Yes, I know it is going to sting me," Hodja laughed. "Almighty Allah created scorpions to sting. But Allah created man with choice. And as for me, I choose to save."

Cheap Donkeys

am ruined, Hodja," Ahmet sobbed into his tea. He glanced mournfully around his well-stocked market stall where his friend Nasreddin Hodja had come to visit. "Half of these goods were destined for the palace, but Emperor Tamerlane has given all my orders to that rogue Osman."

"Osman?" Nasreddin Hodja clucked his tongue in indignation. "His prices may be low but who has ever profited from a bargain with such a merchant? The man waters his wine and weights his scales. Emperor Tamerlane should be told."

Ahmet leaped up and kissed Hodja's hand. "Oh thank you, Hodja!" he beamed. "I knew you would help! May the blessings of Allah go before you. You must come to my house for dinner tonight after you have returned from the palace."

Nasreddin Hodja shook his head as he left and mounted his small donkey. "How wise is the proverb that says, *Listen a hundred times, ponder a thousand times, but speak only once.* My hasty tongue has led me into trouble; let us see if it can lead me back out." Hodja rode to the palace in thoughtful silence, while he considered how to best accomplish his accidental commission.

At the palace, Hodja did not have to wait long for an audience. Indeed, the Emperor eagerly summoned him forward. "Congratulate me, Hodja," the tyrant said with a satisfied grin. "I found fifty new guards before breakfast this morning."

"Truly, my lord is a wonder worthy of contemplation," Hodja answered. "Were these soldiers hiding behind the cheese and olives?"

Tamerlane laughed. "No, my jester of a Hodja. They are the soldiers that I will hire with the money I have saved by buying all my provisions from only the cheapest merchants."

Now Hodja knew that to question a strong man's judgment is to invite the whip or worse, so he said, "My Emperor is the soul of thrift. In that case, I am certain that you will wish to deal with Dursun the donkey seller."

"Dursun?" Tamerlane answered curiously. "I have never heard of him."

"May Allah look away from me if I leave his story hidden from you," Hodja said. The Emperor nodded his assent, and Nasreddin Hodja breathed a silent prayer and began to speak.

"Every market day Dursun would lead a fine donkey through the dusty streets to the bazaar and sell it very cheaply. He grew more and more prosperous while selling his donkeys at prices far below those of the other merchants.

"Eventually his success aroused the curiosity of a certain rich merchant. He cornered Dursun at the market one day and begged for his secret. 'I must know how you can afford to sell your donkeys so cheaply, Dursun effendi. I force my stablehands to work without pay. I also have them steal feed for the donkeys. And yet your prices are still lower than mine!'

"'The explanation is simple,' replied Dursun. 'You only steal food and labor. I steal donkeys.'"

Tamerlane laughed. "Do you claim that all merchants are thieves?"

"Indeed not, my lord," Hodja answered carefully. "Many like the worthy Ahmet are upright men who earn an honest profit on fair dealing. But he who looks only for the cheapest prices may find himself dealing with the greatest thieves."

The Emperor brooded silently for some moments and then protested, "But what of my new soldiers?"

"Give your support to the honest believers in your empire rather than the scoundrels," Hodja answered, "and you will not need more soldiers, my lord."

And so it was that Emperor Tamerlane found fifty soldiers before breakfast only to lose them again by lunch. Nevertheless, he found new wisdom that day, which served him better than an army. May we all share in his good fortune.

The Lost Quilt

ne chilly winter night, Nasreddin Hodja was shaken from sleep by his wife Ayten. "Husband," she whispered anxiously, "I hear a commotion outside. Go and see what it is."

"It is only the howling wind," Hodja said sleepily.

"But I heard shouting," his wife insisted. "I think someone is fighting."

"*May the snake that doesn't bite me live a thousand years,*" Hodja quoted the proverb from beneath his blankets. "It is no concern of ours."

Ayten shook Hodja again, saying, "I will not be able to sleep until I know what is going on."

"Even the dead have peace," Hodja said irritably, "but there is none for the husband of a curious wife." At his wife's continued urging, Hodja wrapped the quilted *yorgan* from the bed around him against the cold night air and went outside to see what was happening. There he found two drunken men quarreling with one another and tried to break it up.

"For shame!" Nasreddin Hodja cried. "What do you mean by fighting at such an hour?"

In response, one of the men snatched the *yorgan* away from Hodja. At the sight of the famous Nasreddin Hodja shivering half-naked in the cold, the men forgot their quarrel and ran off laughing into the night.

Shamefaced, Hodja walked back into the house and slipped back between the warm blankets of his bed.

"What was all the fighting about?" his wife asked.

"Apparently, it was about our *yorgan*," Hodja said, rolling over to sleep. "As soon as they got that, the fight was over."

This story has become proverbial in Turkey. "Yorgan gitti, kavga bitti" (literally, "the quilt is gone, the fight is over") is said whenever a dispute is ended because there is no longer anything to quarrel about.

The Sound of Money

 asreddin Hodja had a tall turban but a short purse, and one day he was walking through the streets of Akshehir with only a piece of bread for his daily meal.

As he passed by a restaurant, he sniffed the mouthwatering aroma of savory *kofte* frying in a pan over a fire. Hoping to capture some of the delicious scent from the meatballs, Hodja held his bread over the pan for a few seconds and then ate it. Afterwards, his poor meal seemed to taste better. The restaurant owner, however, saw Hodja, grabbed him by the neck and angrily demanded that he pay for the meatballs.

Nasreddin Hodja thought for a moment then took a few small coins from his pocket and shook his fist next to the owner's ear so that the coins clinked together.

"What do you think you are doing, Hodja?" the restaurant owner asked curiously.

"I have just paid you for the meatballs," Hodja replied. "Surely the sound of money is fair payment for the smell of food."

Hodja's Sermon

ne day Nasreddin Hodja was asked to deliver the Friday sermon at the mosque. As he ascended the minber to speak, he noticed an elderly goatherd from the mountains in the midst of the assembly. The fact that the goatherd must have journeyed far to hear his words boosted Nasreddin Hodja's confidence a great deal.

As he began to speak, Hodja noticed that the goatherd was particularly attentive to his message. Spurred on by the man's close attention, Nasreddin Hodja spoke with great animation. The goatherd's eyes were fixed on Hodja's face as tears trickled down his grizzled cheeks. By the end of the message, the goatherd had covered his face with his hands and was wailing loudly.

Hodja was moved by the man's passionate piety. Following the namaz prayers, Hodja sought out the goatherd and eagerly asked him which part of his message had so stirred his heart.

"Hodja effendi, I must confess that I did not understand a word of your learned discourse," the goatherd admitted. "I only came here today to seek comfort for the loss of my favorite goat. The sight of your swaying beard reminded me of my poor goat so much that I could not restrain my tears."

Hodja's Prayer

ive times a day, the call to prayer echoed from the minarets of Akshehir. Five times a day Nasreddin Hodja knelt on his well-worn prayer rug, bowing toward Mecca until his forehead touched the ground and speaking his request.

"Oh, Allah, merciful and compassionate! Grant me one hundred gold liras. My creditors will not accept ninety-nine and neither shall I. Send me one hundred—may they come soon."

Day after day, he prayed thus until one day the merchant Osman chanced by Hodja's window and overheard him praying.

"One hundred liras, Allah! Not one coin less than a hundred!"

Osman laughed to himself at Hodja's unconventional prayer. "It is time to put Hodja's piety to the test," thought Osman, who delighted in nothing so much as a good joke.

Returning to his storeroom, Osman counted out ninety-nine liras. He recounted it to be sure there was not a single coin more or less. He put the money in a bag, tied it securely, and tiptoed back to the open window where Hodja was praying.

Taking careful aim, Osman tossed the heavy purse into Nasreddin Hodja's house. The bag barely missed Hodja's bowed head and landed with a merry chink on the floor.

"*Allaha Bin Shukur!* A thousand praises to Allah!" Nasreddin Hodja cried when he saw the bulging purse. He immediately emptied the bag and counted the coins. He counted them again and again. He tried to divide them into ten piles of ten liras each, but, no matter how many times he counted, he was one lira short of his desire.

Osman, peering unseen through the window, clapped his hand tightly over his mouth to hold back his laughter.

"I will let him count once more," Osman said to himself. "Then I will explain the joke to him and we will enjoy a long laugh together."

But Nasreddin Hodja did not count the coins again. Instead, he put them all snugly in the bag and tucked it into his wide belt. Then he knelt on the prayer rug.

"Oh, Allah!" prayed Hodja. "I should have specified that I wanted the one hundred liras together at once. Many thanks for the ninety-nine you did send me. I shall wait patiently for you to send the last one whenever it is convenient."

Hearing this, Osman determined that his joke had gone far enough. He walked to the front of the house and knocked loudly on the door.

When Hodja appeared, Osman grinned and held out his hand.

"The joke is over, Hodja effendi. I should like my gold back now."

"Your gold?" Hodja answered curiously.

"Yes, mine! I tossed the money through the window just for a joke. You said you would not accept less than a hundred liras. I was just trying to show you how foolish such a prayer must sound to Allah."

"*You* tossed it? No, indeed! The money was a gift from Allah. It fell directly from heaven as a reward for my steadfast prayers."

"Enough is enough, Hodja. Do not force me to take you to court for this," said Osman angrily.

"I am quite prepared to submit to the judgment of the court," said Hodja. "You will soon learn that this money fell from heaven."

"*Hadi bakalim!* Let us go now then!" Osman took a step toward the gate, but Hodja hesitated.

"But Ayten is mending my good coat. I cannot come before the kadi like this." Hodja looked down meaningfully at his threadbare clothes.

Osman was determined that no excuse should prevent Nasreddin Hodja from appearing in court. He slipped off his fine silk robe and handsome turban and handed them to Hodja.

"I'll lend you these for the occasion," he said, "but let us hurry to resolve this matter."

"But my donkey! She has a lame foot. I cannot ride her a long distance and, of course, we are in too much of a hurry to walk."

"I'll loan you a horse," Osman answered impatiently.

So Nasreddin Hodja put the clothes on, mounted the merchant's horse, and set off with Osman in his borrowed finery.

Arriving at the courtroom, Osman lost no time in telling his story to the kadi. As he talked, he was disturbed to see Hodja watching him, smiling sadly and shaking his head slowly.

"Well, Nasreddin Hodja," said the kadi, "have you anything to say?"

"Poor Osman effendi," sighed Hodja, his voice heavy with pity. "How sad! How very, very sad! Such a sense of humor and so highly respected by all! To think that he should have lost his mind."

"Lost his mind?" said the kadi. "What do you mean?"

"Oh, didn't you know?" Hodja leaned in toward the kadi and whispered, "He thinks *everything* belongs to him. Watch as I question him."

"Osman effendi," Hodja began, "the horse I rode to court—who does it belong to?"

"It is my horse, of course," exclaimed the merchant.

Hodja shook his head sadly. "And the clothes I am wearing?"

"The clothes are mine as well," cried Osman.

"You see how it is," said the Hodja with a deep sigh of sympathy. "Poor man! No doubt he will claim even the turban on my head as his own."

"Of course I claim the turban," shouted the merchant. "It has always been mine!"

Hodja shrugged his shoulders helplessly. The kadi had evidence enough; let him decide.

"I have heard enough," said the kadi thoughtfully. "I believed Osman Bey about tossing the money bag, though it was a rather wild story. Now I see differently. The pressures of daily commerce and acquisition have clearly unbalanced this man's mind when he claims to own the very clothes on Hodja's back. Osman Bey, I suggest that you go home and take a good long rest. Nasreddin Hodja, you may keep your money bag and all of your possessions that this poor man has tried to take from you in his confusion."

Osman could only sputter in impotent outrage as the kadi dismissed them both from the courtroom. The two men rode in silence through the streets of Akshehir. Osman's shoulders were stooped in defeat.

When Osman reached his own gate, he turned to see a beaming Nasreddin Hodja.

"Here is your money bag," said Hodja, handing the heavy bag to the surprised merchant. "And your clothes. And your horse."

Osman, stared at the smiling Hodja, but could not think of a word to say.

"Wasn't it fun to fool that pompous old kadi?" chuckled the Hodja. "I'm going right back to court to tell him it was all a joke, that things are not always what the evidence makes them seem."

Osman's mute surprise dissolved into helpless mirth as he and Hodja howled with laughter until tears streamed down both their faces.

Before Hodja left, Osman insisted that Hodja keep his clothes and money purse in thanks for the best joke of his life. Hodja then sold the silk robe for the missing lira to repay his debts. So in the end, Osman got his laugh, Hodja got his hundred liras, and Allah answered prayer in a manner that delighted the ears of every good believer. May we all share in their good fortune.

The Larger Fish

 ne hot summer afternoon, Nasreddin Hodja sought refuge from the sun in an ancient stone doorway and found himself inside an Armenian church. Within the cool walls Hodja discovered a worship service already in progress. Not wishing to be rude, he slipped quietly into a seat in the last row and listened with interest.

At the end of the service, the priest came forward to greet Nasreddin Hodja graciously. Hodja complimented the priest on his sermon and invited him to lunch. The priest accepted gladly and they walked arm in arm to a nearby restaurant and ordered fresh fish.

A few minutes later, the waiter brought out a large platter with two cooked fish on it, one of which was quite a bit smaller than the other. Without hesitating, Hodja took the larger fish and put it on his own plate. The priest was offended by Hodja's apparent selfishness and chided him. "I see you were not paying close attention to my sermon."

"On the contrary, my friend," Hodja answered, "I was listening with the utmost attention."

"Then you must have heard Saint Paul's admonition to consider others before yourself," the priest replied.

"Indeed I did," Hodja replied, "and I have taken those words to heart."

Nasreddin Hodja's words incensed the priest who began lecturing him on the evils of greed and pride. Hodja calmly listened to the priest until he paused to draw breath and then asked a question of his own. "If the choice had been yours, what would you have done?"

The priest answered, "I would have considered you first and taken the smaller fish for myself."

"And here you are," Hodja said, placing the smaller fish on the priest's plate. "So why do you fault me for granting your wish?"

The Criticism of Men

nce there was and twice there was not a day when the son of
Nasreddin Hodja came to his father for counsel. Various friends
and relatives had given the boy conflicting advice on a certain
matter, and he wondered, "How can I choose between them without
offending the rest?"

Nasreddin Hodja stroked his beard thoughtfully before answering.
"I believe you will find your answer in Akshehir," he finally said.

The boy was disappointed in his father's response but dutifully loaded
their donkey with some provisions, and the two began walking toward the city.

On the road, they passed a pair of shepherds and overheard them
talking. "Look at those fools walking in the hot sun when they have a
donkey to ride! Surely they should put the animal to good use."

Embarrassed, the son decided the shepherds were right and climbed
onto the donkey until they passed several women walking back from the
marketplace. "For shame," said one woman loudly to another. "A strong
young boy rides the donkey while his aging father has to walk. The boy
should respect his elders and let his father ride."

The son reddened with shame and insisted that Nasreddin Hodja
mount the donkey in his place until they walked by a group of children.
"See how that tyrant Hodja forces his poor son to walk while he rides at
ease like the Emperor himself," they said to one another. "The boy should
ride too."

Stung by their remarks, the boy climbed onto the donkey behind
Nasreddin Hodja until they arrived at the city gates.

"What do you think you're doing?" the gatekeeper chastised them.
"One poor little donkey cannot carry two people on his back. You should
give the animal a rest before you ruin him."

They both dismounted and entered the city just as they had started
with all three walking. Nasreddin Hodja turned to his son and asked,
"Have you found the answer to your question?"

"Yes, father," the son answered. "It is clearly not possible to please everyone.
Therefore, I think I should do what I believe is right and please Allah."

Hodja smiled and said, "May Allah be praised! You have learned in a
day that which has taken me a lifetime."

"The soft sapling can be bent."
(Children can be trained when they are young.)
—Turkish proverb

Alms

t is said that Nasreddin Hodja was once stirred with compassion by the sight of two unfortunate beggars. He searched his pockets for alms and found a large gold coin and a small silver coin. Uncertain how to bestow these gifts, Hodja decided to question the beggars whose eyes hungrily fastened on the coins in his hand.

Noticing the bloodshot eyes of the first beggar, Hodja said, "I see that you are no stranger to alcohol, my son."

"I like to drink raki when I can afford it, Hodja effendi," the first beggar admitted.

Hodja glanced at the man's ample belly. "It seems you enjoy rich food as well."

"I have a taste for sweets," the beggar answered.

"Do you gamble?" Hodja asked, pointing to a pair of worn dice beside him.

"Yes, sir. Whenever I have money," he confessed.

Then Hodja turned to the second beggar, a slender, clear-eyed man. "And do you drink?" he asked.

"May Allah forbid that my lips should touch alcohol, Hodja effendi. I drink nothing but water," he answered.

"Do you eat rich foods?" Hodja asked.

"No, sir. Only bread and olives," he replied modestly.

"And do you gamble?"

"*Allah Korusun*, may Allah protect me from such sin. I spend all my spare time praying at the mosque," he answered, and his companion vouched that it was so.

"Well then," Hodja said, "my duty seems clear." And he handed the gold coin to the fat beggar and the silver coin to the second.

As Nasreddin Hodja walked away, the beggar who received the silver ran after him. "I don't understand, Hodja," he pleaded, "am I not a more worthy recipient of your generosity?"

"My dear brother," Hodja responded gently, "worthiness has nothing to do with it. Alms are given to the needy and, by your own admission, your friend's living expenses are far greater than your own."

The Generous Tip

One sweltering summer day, Nasreddin Hodja went to the *hamam* to refresh himself. When the bath attendants saw his tattered robe and patched sandals, they treated him with contempt, giving him only a small sliver of soap and a dirty scrap of towel. Nevertheless, when he had finished his bath, Hodja gave the workers a shiny gold coin.

The attendants were all amazed because Hodja had not complained about their poor treatment, but had instead given them an exceedingly generous tip. They wondered together how much more he might have given them had they treated him well?

One week later, Hodja came to the *hamam* again. This time the attendants lavished him with every attention. He was skillfully massaged, bathed in heated pools, cleansed with perfumed soaps, and honored like the Emperor himself. When he was finished with his bath, the attendants eagerly awaited their reward, but this time Hodja gave them only one small copper coin of little value.

The disappointed workers were perplexed until Hodja grinned and explained, "This copper coin is for my last visit. The gold coin I gave you last week was for today."

Good Neighbors

ne of Nasreddin Hodja's friends had to return to his home village and asked Hodja to sell his house on the other side of the city for him. Hodja and his wife Ayten went to the house to clean it and meet prospective buyers. Soon after they arrived, a merchant in fine clothes knocked on the front door *tik tik tik*. Hodja invited him in for tea, but the merchant just stood in the doorway.

"Speak quickly, old man, for time is money," he said. "I have in mind to buy this house. But first, tell me about the neighbors. As the proverb says, '*Don't buy a house, buy neighbors.*'"

"You are wise to ask," Nasreddin Hodja answered politely. "May I ask what your current neighbors are like?"

"My neighbors are all selfish, rude, and quick to take offense," the merchant said. "It would be a blessing to escape them."

Nasreddin Hodja nodded his head sadly. "I fear you would find the neighbors here the same."

The merchant scowled in disappointment and stalked off without bidding Hodja good day.

A short time later, a carpenter in threadbare clothes knocked on the front door *tik tik tik*. Hodja invited him inside, and the two chatted together over several glasses of hot tea. After a suitable interval, the carpenter said, "Hodja effendi, I have in mind to buy this house. But first, I wonder if you could tell me about the neighbors? As the proverb says, '*Don't buy a house, buy neighbors.*'"

"You are wise to ask," Nasreddin Hodja answered politely. "May I ask what your current neighbors are like?"

"My neighbors are all warm-hearted, hospitable people and true friends," the carpenter said. "We would be very sad to leave them."

Nasreddin Hodja smiled brightly. "I am confident that you will find the neighbors here to be the same."

The carpenter and Hodja agreed on a price for the house and clasped hands on the deal. After the carpenter had gone, Ayten scolded Hodja saying, "Have you no shame to tell such stories, Nasreddin? You have never even met the neighbors here."

"Nevertheless, I spoke the truth," Hodja answered, "for I have observed that neighbors most often respond in kind, meeting love with love and offense with offense. I am confident that our arrogant merchant is so bad-tempered that he will not find good neighbors anywhere, whereas our humble carpenter will not fail to meet with love wherever he goes."

The Extraordinary Servant

mperor Tamerlane had white teeth but a black heart and his moods were as changeable as the mountain winds. The advisors in his court tried to keep the Emperor's rough temper well oiled with flattery, but one day he grew weary of their incessant compliments.

"If I am the magnificent ruler you say," Tamerlane demanded, "why is my court filled with such commonplace men? Is not an extraordinary leader worthy of extraordinary servants?"

When no one dared answer him, the Emperor erupted in rage. "If someone doesn't do something extraordinary right now," he threatened, "I will cut off the heads of everyone here!"

Nasreddin Hodja wished heartily that he had not visited the court that day. Nevertheless, he bravely stepped forward. "My lord, I'll do something worthy of you."

"And what can you do, Hodja?" Tamerlane demanded.

"I can teach a horse to speak," Hodja answered.

"Excellent," the Emperor answered. "But do not fail me or the pain of your passing will be extraordinary."

"I will do it," said Nasreddin Hodja, "but it will take me five years to accomplish such a feat."

"Granted," said the Emperor. "Choose a horse from my stables and return without fail in five years to show me this wonder."

Some of Tamerlane's chief men sought out Nasreddin Hodja in the stables where they found him climbing onto an aged pack horse.

"Hodja," they said, "we owe you our lives, but can you really teach a horse to speak?"

"No," said Hodja.

"In that case," they said, "you have only earned yourself five years of fearful anxiety, for you will surely be tortured to death in the end."

"You forget that much can happen in five years," Hodja answered. "The Emperor could die. I could die. This horse could die. And who knows," he added with a grin, "perhaps the horse will learn to speak."

Hodja's Dream

asreddin Hodja once had to travel to distant Baghdad. Along the road, Hodja met a dervish mystic and a famous imam. The three companions decided to pool all their resources, sharing the trials and pleasures of the journey together.

One day they met a merchant who tempted them with a single succulent pomegranate. "This is no ordinary fruit," he assured them. "This pomegranate was plucked from the legendary gardens of the Far East, and such is its virtue that whoever eats it shall add ten years to his life."

The three travelers greatly desired this miraculous pomegranate and eagerly poured out their remaining coins to meet the merchant's high price. Afterwards, they fell to arguing over which one of them should eat the fruit. As they walked, each argued his case eloquently, but they were unable to reach agreement.

As the sky darkened into night, they finally agreed that they should pray for revelation and then go to sleep. In the morning, the person who had the most remarkable dream would decide what was to be done.

The next morning, the three arose with the rising sun.

"This was my dream," the dervish began eagerly. "I was drawn deep into the depths of the earth to a place of such peace and serenity that my heart aches to recall it. There I was met by a great company of Allah's holy prophets who said to me, 'You deserve the pomegranate. The purity of your life and devotion to Allah is worthy of imitation, and your example is needed as a bright candle in this dark age of ignorance.'"

"Marvelous indeed," said the imam, "but now you must hear my dream. I was lifted up beyond the clouds into paradise where I was surrounded by brilliant light and inexpressible beauty. An angel came to me and said, 'You deserve the pomegranate. Your learning and pious acts have earned extraordinary merit in heaven, and Allah has destined you to be a leader among men.'"

The dervish and imam then turned to Nasreddin Hodja expectantly. But Hodja admitted frankly that he had received no revelations.

"My brothers, I did not dream but awoke in the middle of the night. When I saw that you were both gone—one into the depths of the earth and the other into the heights of heaven—I praised Allah for rewarding your exemplary piety. Then, seeing that you had each been exalted beyond earthly concerns and had left me alone here in the desert, I saw that there was nothing to do but eat the pomegranate myself. . . so I did."

Nasreddin and the Bully

ven as a young boy, Nasreddin Hodja is said to have demonstrated considerable cleverness. In one such tale, the children of Horto were plagued by a bully everyone called "Ox." Ox had a thick neck, thick arms, and a thick head to match. He spent his days bullying the other boys and bragging about his formidable strength, until one day young Nasreddin drew Ox aside on the school yard.

"Strength is a gift from Allah. But strength by itself is weak," Nasreddin said.

"Oho!" Ox answered, glowering down at the scrawny Nasreddin. "What would a rabbit like you know about strength? I say the strong can do whatever they please."

Nasreddin thought for a moment, then drew a handkerchief from his pocket and pointed to a nearby wall. "Can you throw this cloth over that wall?" he asked.

Ox grinned and snatched the cloth out of Nasreddin's hand. "This is too easy," he said. With a lazy flick, he tossed the cloth toward the wall. But it floated gently down to his toes. With a puzzled look on his face, Ox picked the cloth up, crushed it into a ball and threw it harder. But again, it fluttered to the ground in front of him. Again and again, he grunted and strained to hurl the handkerchief with all his strength only to watch it float to the ground.

Nasreddin watched in silence until a red-faced Ox sullenly threw the handkerchief on the ground. Then he patiently bent down and picked up the cloth.

"Strength by itself is weak," Nasreddin repeated. He picked up a small stone from the ground and wrapped the cloth around it. "But wrap it around humility," he continued, "and it can go much further."

Nasreddin took a firm grip on the cloth-wrapped stone and tossed it. Ox watched the handkerchief sail easily over the wall and then turned back to Nasreddin.

"Remember: Strength with humility goes farther," Nasreddin said and then rejoined the other children in their play.

As Ox turned to watch his schoolfellows, he noticed for the first time how they edged away whenever he caught their eye. His bullying had earned him fear but not friendship.

Ox looked at the stones on the ground. Then he bent down and invited the smallest of the children to climb upon his back for a ride. Soon other children were begging for a turn on his broad shoulders. And when another boy fell and skinned his knee, it was Ox who carried him home to his grateful mother. And so it was, that by the end of the day, Ox had already begun to discover how much farther his strength could go.

In generosity and service be like the flowing river.
In compassion and grace be like the sun.
In concealing others' faults be like the night.
In anger and fury be like the dead.
In modesty and humility be like the earth.
In tolerance be like the sea.
Be as you appear or appear as you are.

——*The Seven Admonitions of Mevlana (thirteenth-century Muslim mystic)*

Tamerlane's Elephant

he irresistible army of the conqueror Tamerlane included many war elephants. Various towns and villages shared the unhappy burden of providing for these hungry beasts, including Nasreddin Hodja's home village of Horto.

One day, a delegation of the village elders visited Nasreddin Hodja and pleaded with him to intercede with Emperor Tamerlane on their behalf.

"Honored Hodja," they begged with one voice. "This elephant has fallen like a curse on our fair village. It destroys our fences, devours our crops, and poisons the very air with its stench. We know that even the terrible Tamerlane respects your wise counsel. Will you not ask him to remove the great beast from our charge so that peace and prosperity may return to Horto?"

When Nasreddin Hodja saw their distress, he was moved with compassion.

"I will serve as your spokesman in this matter," Hodja agreed, "provided that all of you accompany me. I am by no means immune to the great man's wrath and I will require your full support."

The village elders eagerly agreed to this condition and together they traveled to Tamerlane's court with Nasreddin Hodja at the head of the procession. When they reached the Emperor's palace, Nasreddin Hodja wrote his name on the list of petitioners, and they joined the crowd waiting outside the court.

When the village elders saw the red-faced Emperor Tamerlane, their hearts melted. They watched as a drought-stricken farmer pleaded to be excused from taxes only to be punished with forty lashes before their eyes. In the face of such cruelty, they began to think differently of their errand.

At last Nasreddin Hodja's name was called and he bravely pressed forward to plead the village's case. The elders, however, dared not follow him. Instead, they quietly slipped away among the crowd.

When he reached the Emperor's throne, Nasreddin Hodja confidently began his rehearsed speech: "O Exalted Emperor, I have a request regarding one of your elephants on behalf of your humble servants in Horto..." Hodja swept his arm backward to indicate the village elders who should have been behind him. Realizing that the villagers had abandoned him before the ruthless ruler, Nasreddin Hodja improvised quickly without skipping a beat. "The village elders wish me to say that the elephant you have quartered in their village is lonely and requires a partner to be happy."

Emperor Tamerlane was delighted with this suggestion and promised to send a second elephant to the village immediately.

How Long Will it Take?

ne afternoon Nasreddin Hodja was walking along the village road when he met another traveler, a stranger to that neighborhood, resting beside the road.

"*Selamunaleykum*, peace be with you, effendi," the stranger greeted him. "Can you please tell me how long it is to the next village?"

Nasreddin Hodja looked at the traveler and answered, "*Aleykumselam*, peace be upon you. I am afraid I cannot say how long it will take you."

The puzzled stranger asked, "Isn't this the road to the village?"

"Yes," the Hodja answered, "I have just come from the village."

"Then how long will it take me to get there?" the stranger repeated impatiently.

"I cannot say," Hodja answered.

Irritated, the traveler muttered to himself, "A white beard could mean either wisdom or senility. Perhaps this poor old fool is simpleminded." He repeated his question slowly, using hand gestures for emphasis. "How—long—to—the—next—village?"

Nasreddin Hodja smiled in amusement and answered, "I—can—not—say."

The frustrated traveler pushed past Hodja and began to walk with great strides down the village road. After watching him for a few moments, Hodja called out, "My friend, it will take you no longer than an hour to reach the village."

The traveler stopped. "Why didn't you tell me that before?" he yelled in exasperation.

"How could I say," Hodja answered calmly, "until I saw how fast you planned to walk?"

Four Arrows

t was a bright spring day when Tamerlane asked Nasreddin Hodja to go with him to the pasture where his soldiers were at their archery practice. It was the sort of day when a man feels as bold as the sunshine and as quick as the wind. By the time they joined the soldiers, Hodja was no longer an elderly scholar. On this day, he was a daring hero, a man who could do anything.

"Not bad," said Hodja as one soldier's arrow neatly skewered its target. "The youth has some skill. Of course, when I used to shoot—"

"You were an archer?" Tamerlane looked at Hodja in surprise.

"Indeed I was!" Hodja answered airily. On a day like this, he felt could be anything. "I was a famous champion in my day. Men would come from far off to see my skill."

Emperor Tamerlane beckoned to the nearest soldier. "My soldiers need to see some good shooting," he said as he took the bow and arrows from the man. "Here is your chance to show us how it really should be done." Tamerlane held out the bow and arrow toward Nasreddin Hodja.

"I would not wish to embarrass your men with such a display while they are still learning," Hodja answered humbly as he cast about for a way to decline this unwelcome invitation. "Let us not discourage them."

"Nonsense!" Tamerlane answered as he held the bow toward the squirming Hodja. "I'm certain they will be inspired to greater efforts by your skill."

"It is so long since I have worked at archery," hedged Nasreddin Hodja. "It might be better not to do it today."

"Oh, your hands will remember their old skill as soon as they grip the bow." Tamerlane pulled back the bowstring and sent an arrow whizzing into a target within two hairs of the bull's-eye. "Look! I have not touched bow or arrow for months, but I feel as though I had been shooting yesterday."

"But there is an ache in my shoulder that has been bothering me all winter," Hodja protested.

"I thought you said this morning that the warm sunshine had baked out that pain," Tamerlane answered as he extended the bow and a fresh arrow.

Nasreddin Hodja knew a command when he saw it and dared not press the Emperor's patience further. He could do no more than try.

"Ah yes, well let's get to it then!" Hodja tried to conjure up a confident air as he awkwardly accepted the big bow. A quick glance at one of the archers showed him which way to hold it. After two or three tries, he had the arrow fitted into something close to the right position. Hodja squinted at the target, took careful aim, and released the arrow. It wavered and fell just a short distance ahead of him.

To Tamerlane's surprise, Hodja showed no hint of anger or embarrassment at his feeble shot. His confident grin was firmly in place.

"That, sire," Hodja laughed, "is to show you how your huntsmen shoot."

Nasreddin Hodja took another arrow from the soldier's quiver. He beamed pleasantly at the little group of soldiers that was quickly gathering to watch his antics. He put his second arrow in place, gave a mighty pull on the string, and sent the arrow whizzing high into the air. Soldiers leaped out of the way as it fell to the ground.

"And that," said the Hodja with a cheerful nod, "is to show you how your captains shoot."

Nasreddin Hodja took a third arrow and adjusted it. The soldiers drew back anxiously. It was well that they did for the third arrow wobbled far to the right of the mark.

"And that," said the Hodja carelessly, "is to show you how your generals shoot."

Nasreddin Hodja took a fourth arrow. He no longer bothered to squint at the target. He merely put the arrow to the bowstring, gave a yank, and let it go where it would. Surely Allah guided his aim. for this time the arrow leaped forward with a whirr to lodge itself neatly in the center of the bull's-eye.

For a moment, Hodja stared wide-eyed at his arrow quivering in the target. Then he recovered his composure. "And *that*," he said triumphantly, "is how Nasreddin Hodja shoots."

Dawn

One chill night, in the twilight of his life, Nasreddin Hodja warmed his gnarled hands at the fireplace of the local teahouse. A bearded muezzin beside Hodja squinted down his nose at a boisterous farmer in the corner laughing loudly with friends over hot tea. "Listen to that worldly fool," he remarked. "It is obvious that there is no fear of Allah in that empty head."

"You should look again," Hodja said quietly. "I believe you have overlooked something."

The muezzin was startled by this mild rebuke and looked again at the farmer to see what he had missed. Was he perhaps wearing the white cap of one who had made the pilgrimage to Mecca? In the dim light, the muezzin couldn't be certain.

A sharp-eyed merchant on Hodja's left cast an appraising look toward the farmer and offered his own assessment. "I cannot speak to his faith," the merchant said confidently, "but I know an easy mark when I see one. Look at those patched clothes. I'd wager the fool has never come out on the winning end of a bargain in his life. Perhaps I should invite him to visit my market stall."

"Very perceptive," Hodja answered, "but like the esteemed muezzin, I believe you too have missed a vital detail."

The merchant scowled at the thought he might have erred. What did Nasreddin Hodja see that he could have overlooked? Surely he would have noticed a bulging purse or some other sign of prosperity? Or would he? The flickering light of the hearth barely reached that corner.

"I wonder that you can see anything in this light, Hodja," the merchant finally said. "I daresay the matter would be clear to us both in the light of day."

"Indeed darkness confuses all," Nasreddin Hodja said. "But how will you know when the darkness has ended and the dawn has begun?"

The muezzin answered, "I know the night is over and the dawn has come when I can tell the difference between a white and a black thread in my hand."

Nasreddin Hodja shook his head. "It is an answer straight from the holy books," he replied, "but Allah teaches a better one."

Then the merchant ventured a guess. "I know you are a man of the world, Hodja. Surely you will agree that the dawn has come when one can discern the difference between a gold coin and a silver coin on the counter at the bazaar."

"Many consider you wealthy, my friend," Hodja said sadly, "but your answer marks you as poorer than you know."

The muezzin and the merchant stared silently into the fire for some time. Finally, they blurted out, "Don't leave us in suspense, Hodja! Give us the solution to your riddle, for we can think of no other answers."

Nasreddin Hodja turned and held them both with his eyes as he spoke. "When you look into the eyes of a human being and see a brother or sister rather than an object of condemnation or a chance of profit, then you will know that dawn has come. If you cannot see a brother or sister, you will know that you are still in darkness."

About the Author

Michael Shelton grew up in Massachusetts, where his father's bedtime stories of "The Great Wazumba" and "Bulgy Bear" sparked a lifetime love of storytelling. In 2001, Mike and his wife Joann took a surprising leap of faith and relocated to Turkey where they found wonderful neighbors, adopted six beautiful Turkish daughters, and uncovered a treasure trove of folktales waiting to be retold.

Mike is a freelance writer, translator, and occasional editor. This is his first folktale collection. When Mike isn't collecting stories, he enjoys crafting his own, baking cookies, and surfing the oceans of emotions flowing through his household of seven amazing ladies.

Made in United States
North Haven, CT
22 August 2022